RAPID REFERENCE GUIDE TO

QuarkXPress®

QuarkXPress®

Michael Fraase

BUSINESS ONE IRWIN
Homewood, Illinois 60430

Business One Irwin professional books are available for bulk sales at quantity discounts. For information, please contact Marketing Manager, Professional Books Group, Business One Irwin, 1818 Ridge Road, Homewood, IL 60430.

This publication is designed to provide accurate and authoritative information in regard to the subject matter covered. It is sold with the understanding that neither the author nor the publisher is engaged in rendering legal, accounting, or other professional service. If legal advice or other expert assistance is required, the services of a competent professional person should be sought.

From a Declaration of Principles jointly adopted by a Committee of the American Bar Association and a Committee of Publishers.

Senior editor: Susan Stevens, Ph.D.
Project editor: Karen J. Nelson
Production manager: Mary Jo Parke
Designer: Michael Fraase
Printer: R. R. Donnelley & Sons Company

Library of Congress Cataloging-in-Publication Data
Fraase, Michael.
    Rapid reference guide to QuarkXPress / Michael Fraase.
        p.   cm.—(The Business One Irwin rapid reference series)
    Includes index.
    ISBN 1–55623–740–5
    1. QuarkXPress (Computer file) 2. Desktop publishing—Computer programs   I. Title. II. Title: QuarkXPress. III. Series.
    Z286.D47F728   1993
    686.2'2544536—dc20   92–27700

Printed in the United States of America

1 2 3 4 5 6 7 8 9 0 DOC 9 8 7 6 5 4 3 2

Trademark Credits

All terms mentioned in this work that are known to be trademarks or service marks are listed below. In addition, terms suspected of being trademarks or service marks have been appropriately capitalized. Use of a term in this work should not be regarded as affecting the validity of any trademark or service mark.

Adobe, Illustrator, and PostScript are registered trademarks of Adobe Systems Inc.

Adobe Type Manager, ATM, and the ATM logo are trademarks of Adobe Systems Inc.

Aldus, the Aldus logo, and PageMaker are registered trademarks of Aldus Corporation.

Apple, the Apple logo, AppleTalk, HyperCard, ImageWriter, LaserWriter, and Macintosh are registered trademarks of Apple Computer Inc.

AppleCD, Apple Desktop Bus, AppleMouse, AppleShare, A/UX, EtherTalk, Finder, FinePrint, HyperTalk, LocalTalk, PhotoGrade, QuickDraw, and TrueType are trademarks of Apple Computer Inc.

Arts & Farces and the Arts & Farces logo are trademarks of Arts & Farces.

Introduction

In 1985 Apple Computer introduced the first PostScript laser printer, the LaserWriter. That same year Aldus Corporation released the first version of its PageMaker page layout software. At that time Paul Brainerd, founder of Aldus, coined the term "desktop publishing."

Desktop publishing has clearly moved into the publishing mainstream. Although the pioneering days of desktop publishing are over, we are continually confronted with the challenges of charting new territory as the technological tools for layout, illustration, typography, color prepress, and printing continue to evolve.

Denver, Colo.-based Quark Inc. released the first version of QuarkXpress in 1987. Early versions of the software were notoriously complex. Version 3.0 offered a completely redesigned user interface that made the software much easier to use.

QuarkXPress has helped change the way publishers publish information, and you can see its impact virtually everywhere you look. If you were to take a sample of magazines and newspapers—mainstream as well as specialized—you would have a fairly safe bet that many of them were produced using QuarkXPress on the Macintosh.

Who Can Use This Book

This book is intended for anyone who is currently using or contemplating the use of QuarkXPress. This book will benefit two types of users:

- Individuals or workgroup members who have basic experience with another page layout or design program.

- Individuals who need to create simple page layouts within QuarkXPress.

This book is not meant to be a replacement for the QuarkXPress documentation set. Nor is this book intended to replace the wide variety of books and other information available for using QuarkXPress or designing for print publication.

I'm assuming that you have at least a passing acquaintance with things Macintosh; that you know how to click and double-click on screen items and that you understand the basic Macintosh operating conventions.

I'm not assuming that you're an expert, but I am assuming that you have read at least the most basic parts of the documentation set that came with your computer and with QuarkXPress. If you haven't, it's OK; go and do it now. This book will still be here when you get back.

About the Series

This book is part of the Business One Irwin Rapid Reference series. Each is designed basically the same way, and with the same intention: to provide coverage of the basic functionality of leading software applications for the Apple Macintosh family of computers.

The underlying idea for this series is that most people are far too busy to wade through enormous amounts of documentation, and that they shouldn't have to; at least not to perform basic tasks within the product.

Each book in this series covers the basic functionality of the product at hand.

The underlying idea at work here is that basic information will enable you to become productive quickly, allowing you to explore the deeper levels of a program's functionality later, when you have more time.

A wide variety of titles is currently under development. If there are specific titles you would like to see, please don't hesitate to contact the publisher or the author.

Business One Irwin
1818 Ridge Road
Homewood, IL 60430
800/634-3966

Michael Fraase
Arts & Farces
2285 Stewart Avenue
Suite 1315
Saint Paul, MN 55116
612/698-0741

Navigating This Book

This book, like the others in the Rapid Reference series, is organized in a series of relatively short chapters for brevity and easy navigation.

The material is thoroughly cross-referenced wherever possible, and a complete table of contents and index are provided.

Conventions Used in This Book

Each title in the Rapid Reference series contains various tips, warnings, and items flagged for your consideration. These items are represented graphically throughout the entire series using the following conventions:

The **checkmark** is used to mark an item for your consideration. It is recommended that you consider this information before going any further in the process described. Items marked with the **checkmark** are important to consider, but will not cause any serious problems if you ignore or disregard them. The checkmark is also used to identify undocumented features as well as tips and shortcuts.

The familiar **caution** icon is used in a manner consistent with Apple's documentation and human user interface guidelines. The **caution** icon is used throughout this book to call your attention to an operation that may have undesirable results if completed.

The **stop** icon is used in a manner consistent with Apple's documentation and human user interface guidelines. The **stop** icon is used to call your attention to an operation that can cause a serious problem. The **stop** icon is used only for information that can cause serious and sometimes irreparable damage. Pay close attention to any stop icons.

Table of Contents

CHAPTER ONE: What's New in v3.1?

CHAPTER TWO: Installing QuarkXPress

CHAPTER THREE: QuarkXPress Basics

CHAPTER FOUR: Working With Text

CHAPTER FIVE: Working With Graphics

INDEX

What's New in QuarkXPress v3.1?

Contrary to its incremental version number, QuarkXPress v3.1 is a fairly significant update to one of the leading page layout software packages for the Macintosh. QuarkXPress has continued to evolve from a quirky and unstable product to a remarkably stable publishing workhorse.

If you produce newspapers, magazines, or other short, design-intensive publications, Quark-XPress v3.1 is one of the most powerful software tools you can buy.

System 7 Support

QuarkXPress v3.1 is System 7 "savvy," fully supporting the crucial aspects of System 7 including 32-bit addressing, the core suite of AppleEvents, and virtual memory.

You can use System 7's Publish and Subscribe functionality within QuarkXPress to subscribe to any editions published by other software programs. The support provided for editions is almost identical to the program's element linking. In fact, since QuarkXPress supports only PICT-format edition files, you're better off using the Auto Picture Import feature of QuarkXPress.

The TrueType font format is supported, although better results can almost always be obtained by using Type 1 PostScript fonts.

Edition Support

Although QuarkXPress doesn't support the Publish features of System 7's Publish and Subscribe, you can subscribe to *Edition files* that have been published by other Macintosh software programs that support Publish and Subscribe.

The ability to subscribe to Edition files created by other software programs is best seen as an alternative to the product's traditional support of linked files.

The difference is that information published within another Mac program creates a separate edition file; the linking support of QuarkXPress does not need an intermediate file.

System 7's Publish and Subscribe capability is a logical extension to the information transfer capabilities inherent in the Clipboard, automating the exchange of information between documents. It's easiest to think of Publish and Subscribe as a *live* Copy and Paste.

To initiate Publish and Subscribe you *publish* a document (or a section of a document), resulting in the creation of an *Edition* file. You (or other workgroup members with access to the edition file) *subscribe* to the edition, automatically inserting its information into other documents. When the linking has been completed, changes to the original document are propagated to the subscribing documents automatically.

Documents do not have to be open in order to receive edition updates. Edition updates are forwarded automatically the next time the document is opened.

System 7's Publish and Subscribe capabilities also work in a seamless manner across a local area network. Edition updates are stored on non-shared disks and are automatically forwarded to the appropriate subscribers the next time you share the volume or folder.

Creating a Subscriber

You can create a Subscriber within QuarkXPress with the following steps.

Select the Subscribe to... command from the Edit menu. The Subscriber dialog box, shown in Figure 1, will be displayed.

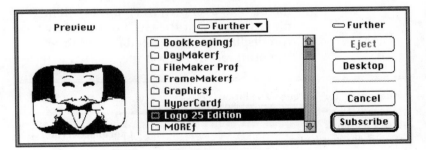

Figure 1   Subscriber dialog box.

1. Navigate to the Edition to which you want to subscribe within the Subscriber dialog box.

2. Select the Edition file.

3. Click the **Subscribe** button. The Subscriber will be created and displayed at the center of your screen.

4. Drag the Subscriber to position it within your QuarkXPress document.

Setting Subscriber Options

Subscriber options are available for any Edition file. These controls allow you to launch the software program that published the Edition file, cancel the Subscriber, and specify how and when Edition file updates occur.

You can set the Edition file updating options within QuarkXPress with these steps.

1. Select the Subscriber you want to edit within your QuarkXPress document. Selection handles will appear around the Subscriber, indicating that it has been selected.

2. Select the Subscriber options... command from the Edit menu. The Subscriber options dialog box, as shown in Figure 2, will be displayed. Note that the **Get Edition Now** button displays the creation date and time of the most recent Edition file.

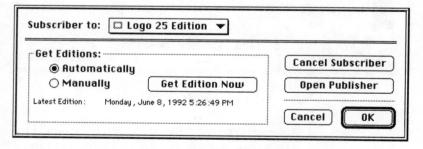

Figure 2   Subscriber options dialog box.

3. Select the option representing how you want the Edition file to be updated within the Subscriber with the Get Editions radio button.

- Click the **Automatically** radio button to automatically update the Edition file each time the document is opened.

- Click the **Manually** radio button to update the Edition file only when you click the **Get Edition Now** button.

4. Click the **Cancel Subscriber** button to cancel the link to the current Edition file.

5. Click the **Open Publisher** button to launch the software program that published the Edition file.

Click the **OK** button. The Subscriber will be updated to reflect your changes

XPress Preferences

QuarkXPress no longer creates the XPress Data file; the settings are now contained within the XPress Preferences file.

Important information—such as kerning tables, tracking tables, custom frames, and hyphenation exceptions—is stored in both the XPress Preferences file and the document itself.

No longer do you have to remember to include your XPress Data file with your document to the service bureau.

In addition, several new preference controls have been added.

Application Preferences

You set the QuarkXPress Application preferences by selecting the Application... command from the Preferences hierarchical menu on the Edit menu. Doing so causes the Application Preferences dialog box, shown in Figure 3 to appear.

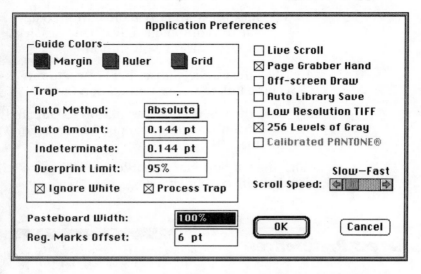

Figure 3   *Application Preferences dialog box.*

Guide Colors

Clicking any of the three available **Guide Colors** buttons in the upper left portion of the Application Preferences dialog box displays the familiar Macintosh color wheel in a dialog box. You can select a color by clicking anywhere within the color wheel or you can enter numerical values for the desired color in the available fields.

- *Margin guides* indicate the page margins.

- *Ruler guides* are the horizontal or vertical guides that you can pull out onto the page.

- *Grid guides* are displayed only when you select the Show Baseline Grid command from the View menu. They indicate the document's grid formed by the baselines.

Live Scroll

When you drag either of the scroll boxes within the horizontal or vertical scroll bars, no visual feedback about the scrolling area is ordinarily provided. If you hold down the Option key while moving the scroll box, the QuarkXPress window is continually updated as you scroll, providing visual navigation feedback. This feature is called *live scrolling.*

If you check the **Live Scroll** checkbox in the Application Preferences dialog box, live scrolling is active without holding the Option key.

Page Grabber Hand

The QuarkXPress Page Grabber Hand offers a more intuitive option to live scrolling. If you check the **Page Grabber Hand** checkbox and hold down the Option key, click anywhere within the QuarkXPress window, and drag, the screen moves in the direction of the drag motion.

Alternatively, if you uncheck the **Page Grabber Hand** checkbox, Option-clicking anywhere within the QuarkXPress window toggles between the Actual Size view and the Fit in Window view with each Option-click.

Off-screen Draw

Checking the **Off-screen Draw** checkbox causes QuarkXPress to redraw all the elements on a page before displaying the page on screen. If you uncheck the checkbox, the page elements are displayed as they are redrawn. There is no advantage in enabling this option; it takes just as long to redraw the screen with either method.

Auto Library Save

QuarkXPress Libraries are usually saved only when you specifically close them. If you check the **Auto Library Save** checkbox, the Library is saved whenever you add an item to it. This slows down the program's performance somewhat, but offers the benefit of added safety when you are adding Library items.

More information about Libraries is provided in the Library Palette section beginning on page 56.

Low Resolution TIFF

TIFF-format graphic images are ordinarily displayed at a default resolution of 72-dots-per-inch. Checking the **Low Resolution TIFF** checkbox causes the default display resolution for TIFF images to be reduced to 36 dpi. This results in a significantly faster screen redraw.

You can override the **Low Resolution TIFF** checkbox setting by holding the Shift key down while you import a TIFF image. Holding the Shift key down with the **Low Resolution TIFF** checkbox checked results in a 72 dpi screen image. Holding the Shift key down with the **Low Resolution TIFF** checkbox unchecked results in a 36 dpi screen image.

256 Levels of Gray

QuarkXPress ordinarily displays 8-bit grayscale (256 shades of gray) images with only 16 shades of gray (4-bit display). Checking the **256 Levels of Gray** checkbox in the Applications Preferences dialog box causes 8-bit grayscale images to be displayed with the full 256 shades of gray.

Checking the **256 Levels of Gray** checkbox causes the screen redraw to be significantly slower, but the displayed images are of much higher quality. This setting has no effect on the way the images will appear when printed; it only affects the how the images appear on the screen.

Calibrated Pantone

If you check the **Calibrated Pantone** checkbox in the Application Preferences dialog box, QuarkXPress will display up to six Pantone colors using the updated Pantone color set provided by the Professional Color Toolkit.

In order to use this feature, you must have a monitor and video card capable of displaying at least 8-bits (256 shades) of color and the Professional Color Toolkit. The Toolkit is distributed free of charge by user groups and online communications services.

This feature is not of much use, since it is foolhardy to rely on a computer screen for an accurate representation of any printed color. This is primarily a result of the differences inherent in the way color is displayed on the computer monitor and the way it is printed on paper. More information is provided in the Working With Color section beginning on page 87.

Scroll Speed

The Scroll Speed control allows you to customize how fast QuarkXPress scrolls the window when you use either the horizontal or vertical scroll bar. A faster Scroll Speed allows you to navigate through your pages faster, at the expense of a more precise level of control.

Pasteboard Width

The Pasteboard is the area around the outside of each page of your document. You can use this area to bleed elements off the page as well as a temporary storage area for elements such as graphic elements, cut lines, rules, and boxes.

The Pasteboard Width field allows you to specify a width—as a percentage of one page of your document—for the QuarkXPress pasteboard. Entering 100% in this field results in a Pasteboard that is as wide as a page of your document. Entering 50% in this field results in a Pasteboard that is one-half as wide as the page. There is no way to specify the height of the Pasteboard.

Reg. Marks Offset

Registration marks are a group of related page elements that QuarkXPress automatically places outside of the page boundaries of each page of your document. When printed, they provide important information about each page.

Crop marks define the boundaries of each page of your document and appear outside each corner of the page. They indicate where the page should be cut.

Registration marks provide information about how each color plate aligns with the others when it is printed. They appear along each side of the page and are used by the stripper to align, or "register" each plate when printing color.

The Reg. Marks Offset field in the Application Preferences dialog box allow you to control how far out—in points—the registration marks will print. This is especially useful when your pages will be cut on a high-speed cutting machine.

Trap

The Trap section of the Application Preferences dialog box allow you to control QuarkXPress's color trapping function. This area of the dialog box is subdivided into six specific controls.

Auto Method

The Auto Method determines how automatic trapping should be handled and is specified by selecting one of two commands from the associated pop-up menu.

The Proportional command determines the width of the trap by which color is darker and its level of darkness. The maximum trap amount is the value contained in the Auto Amount field.

The Absolute command specifies that the same trapping value—the value contained in the Auto Amount field—is always used. This is usually the most appropriate choice for automatic trapping.

Auto Amount

The value contained in this field determines the maximum value that Proportional automatic trapping uses and the exact value used by Absolute automatic trapping.

Indeterminate

The value contained in this field is the absolute amount of trap to be used for elements that overlap indeterminate colors. A background color is said to be indeterminate if it contains more than one color. A blue box that partially overlaps a green box on a white page, for example, would be seen by QuarkXPress as having an indeterminate background because the background would contain elements that were more than one color—the green box and the white page.

More information is provided in the Ignore White section, below.

Overprint Limit

The Overprint Limit field contains a percentage value that is used by QuarkXPress to determine which color to overprint in addition to black. QuarkXPress will overprint any color with a tint level that is above the Overprint Limit specified in this field.

If the color is screened to a tint level that is lower than the Overprint Limit specification, the color will be knocked out rather than overprinted.

Ignore White

You can check the **Ignore White** checkbox to exert a finer level of control over how QuarkXPress deals with indeterminate color.

QuarkXPress determines a color to be indeterminate when it gets confused, as in the case of a blue box that partially overlaps a green box on a white page in the example used above in the Indeterminate section.

In this case, checking the **Ignore White** checkbox would cause QuarkXPress to completely ignore the overlapping white background and the color of the green box would no longer be seen as indeterminate.

This only works with indeterminate colors that include white as a factor.

Process Trap

Checking the **Process Trap** checkbox in the Application Preferences dialog box causes Quark-XPress to spread or choke certain process colors, resulting in better process color trapping.

Any foreground process color that is darker than the same color in a background element is spread by one-half of the trapping value. Similarly any foreground process color that is lighter than the same color in a background element is choked by one-half of the trapping value.

Typographic Preferences

Typographic preferences are specified by selecting the Typographic... command from the Preferences hierarchical menu on the Edit menu. Doing so causes the Typographic Preferences dialog box, shown in Figure 4 to appear.

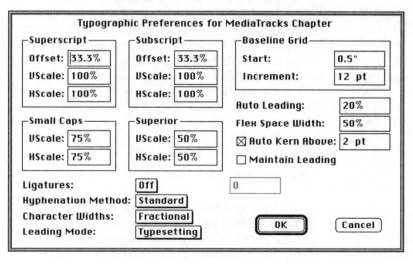

Figure 4   Typographic Preferences dialog box.

Three new Typographic preference settings have been added to QuarkXPress 3.1.

Flex Space Width

A flex space is a customizable space character with an adjustable, fixed width. Because a flex space is a fixed width character, it retains its width even in justified text.

You enter a flex space by typing Option-Shift-space from the keyboard.

You can specify the width for the flex space by entering a value—as a percentage of an en space—in the Flex Space Width field within the Typographic Preferences dialog box.

Maintain Leading

Checking the **Maintain Leading** checkbox in the Typographic Preferences dialog box causes QuarkXPress to maintain the leading value of each line within a text box. The leading value of the lines is maintained even if another page element—such as a picture box—overlaps the text and causes the lines to be moved. This setting ensures that the leading grid is maintained consistently throughout the document.

Enhanced Hyphenation

The hyphenation feature of QuarkXPress has been updated to include an Enhanced item on the Hyphenation Method pop-up menu. Selecting this item causes the program to use a newer hyphenation scheme that breaks complex words more appropriately.

New Palettes

Three new palettes have been added to the QuarkXPress environment. These new palettes are intuitive and easily mastered. Using them will boost your productivity considerably.

Trap Information Palette

QuarkXPress 3.1 includes the capability to trap a specific object to its background rather than simply trapping one color to another. The Trap Information palette, shown in Figure 5, provides the current trap information for any selected page element and lets you modify that object's trap value.

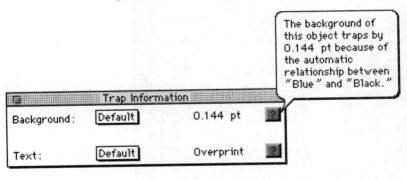

Figure 5   Trap Information palette.

As you can see, explanatory help is also available by clicking on the **Question Mark (?)** button.

You can override the default settings for the selected object's trapping by selecting a command from those available on two pop-up menus. The pop-up menu labels change based on the type of object that is currently selected.

Menu items available are Overprint, Knockout, Auto Amount (+), Auto Amount (-), and Custom.

The Auto Amount commands are based on the value in the Auto Amount field of the Application Preferences dialog box, explained in the Auto Amount section on page 11.

If you select the Custom command, a field appears, in which you can enter any trap value between -36 points and +36 points.

Style Sheets Palette

The Style Sheets palette, shown in Figure 6, contains a scrolling list of all the defined paragraph styles in the current document.

Style names —

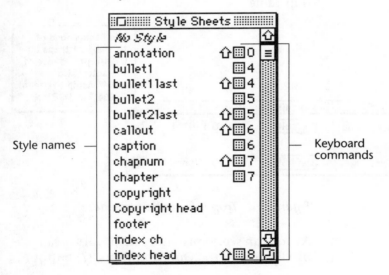

— Keyboard commands

Figure 6   Style Sheets palette.

You can use the items listed in the Style Sheets palette to assign a style to the current paragraph by clicking on the style's name.

You can edit any existing style by Command-clicking on its name in the Style Sheets Palette. Doing so causes the Style Sheets dialog box to appear with the style's name highlighted.

The current definition for the style appears in the lower portion of the dialog box.

You can edit the style by clicking the **Edit** button and using the controls within the Edit Style Sheet dialog box.

More information on creating, editing, and using style sheets is provided in the Paragraph Formatting section, beginning on page 64.

Colors Palette

A Colors palette has also been added to the QuarkXPress environment. This palette, shown in Figure 7, allows you to apply and edit colors with a single click.

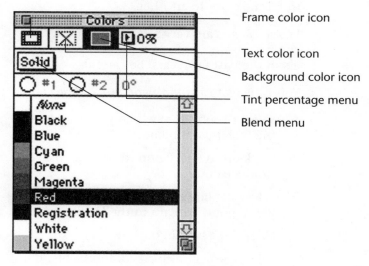

Frame color icon

Text color icon

Background color icon

Tint percentage menu

Blend menu

Figure 7   Colors palette.

The Colors palette contains a scrolling list of every available color. Also available within the palette is a pop-up menu to control the Tint Percentage for the selected object.

To apply color to an object, use these steps.

1. Click on the correct icon for the aspect of the object you want to change.

2. Select the desired color by selecting its name from the scrolling list.

3. If you want a tint for the color, select the item representing the percentage of the tint from the Tint Percentage pop-up menu.

4. Press the Return key to apply the change.

Linear Blends

A Linear Blend feature has been added to Quark-XPress 3.1. A linear blend, also known as a graduated fill, allows you to blend an object's color from one color to another.

Linear blends are very attractive but have become somewhat overused by electronic designers in the past few years. Be careful.

You can create a color blend with these steps.

1. Select the object to which you want to apply the linear color blend.

2. Click on the Background color icon in the Colors palette.

3. Select the Linear Blend command from the Blend pop-up menu in the Colors palette.

4. Click the #1 radio button.

5. Select the beginning color for the blend from the scrolling list.

6. Select a tint percentage if necessary.

7. Click the **#2** radio button.

8. Select the ending color for the blend from the scrolling list.

9. Select a tint percentage if necessary.

10. Specify the angle for the blend as a degree increment from 0 to 359.

   - The default of zero degrees places the beginning blend color on the left and the ending blend color on the right. Increasing the degree increment rotates the blend counter-clockwise.

The blend will appear on the screen.

You can change either of the blend colors by repeating steps 4–6 and/or 7–9 as needed.

Minor Enhancements

Some of QuarkXPress 3.1's new features appear relatively minor at first glance. If you are working in a production environment, however, these subtle new features become quite powerful.

Intelligent Screen Zoom

Selecting a magnification percentage from the View menu now causes QuarkXPress to zoom in or out to the desired percentage while at the same time centering the current page or two-page spread within the document window.

If a whole page or spread won't fit on your display, the active area is centered on your screen.

Picture Preview

A Picture Preview feature has been added to the Get Picture dialog box, as shown in Figure 8.

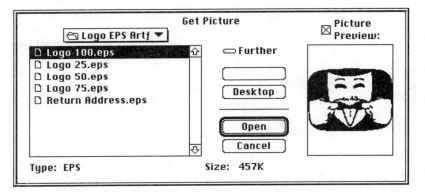

Figure 8   Get Picture dialog box.

Checking the **Picture Preview** checkbox and selecting a graphic file in the scrolling list causes a preview of the graphic to be displayed within the right panel of the Get Picture dialog box. This is useful for locating graphic images that you have misnamed or misplaced.

The Picture Preview can be painfully slow to appear on very complex graphic images. It is best to uncheck the Picture Preview checkbox in most cases, using it only when you need to find something. The Picture Preview may be pretty to look at, and very useful when needed, but it really slows things down in a production environment.

Rapid Font Change

You can quickly change your font selection by pressing Command-Shift-Option-M. This combination of keystrokes places the cursor in the Font field of the Measurements palette.

If you were using any version of Suitcase with QuarkXPress prior to version 3.1 and forgot to open the appropriate typefaces you would have to quit QuarkXPress, open the typefaces, and then re-launch QuarkXPress. This is no longer necessary. QuarkXPress can now use any font as soon as it is opened by Suitcase.

Single Word Justify

Users who design and layout newspapers with QuarkXPress will find use for the new **Single Word Justify** checkbox in the Hyphenation & Justification dialog box. When checked, this feature causes QuarkXPress to force the justification of a single word on a line by itself.

Newspaper designers will undoubtedly love this feature, and its use is arguably acceptable in most newspapers. Be careful using Single Word Justify in most other types of documents, however. It can rarely be used effectively and will be immediately apparent to even the untrained eye.

Automatic Ligatures

QuarkXPress 3.1 automatically inserts ligatures for the "fi" and "fl" letterpairs. Ligatures are specialized characters that appear to be two letters touching, creating an appearance that is more aesthetically appealing.

Ligatures can be edited, and the spelling checker now handles ligatures appropriately (it doesn't flag them as misspelled words).

A Ligatures pop-up menu and field have been added to the Typographic Preferences dialog box, as shown in Figure 9.

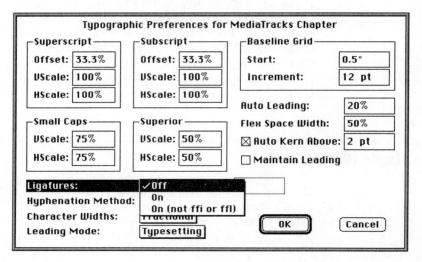

Figure 9   *Ligatures pop-up menu in Typographic Preferences dialog box.*

The Typographic Preferences dialog box contains a new ligature field that allows you to specify a tracking or kerning level above which Quark-XPress will split the ligature.

Entering a 3 in the ligature field, for example, causes the ligature to be maintained until tracking or kerning reaches 4 units.

Each unit is 1/200th of an em.

Enhanced Ruler Guides

Ruler guides are much easier to move in the new version of QuarkXPress. Clicking on any visible ruler guide with the Item tool now allows you to move the guide even if surrounding page elements overlap the ruler guide.

Similarly, you can Option-click on either ruler to remove all ruler guides associated with that ruler.

The QuarkXPress rulers are finally visually accurate (they weren't in previous versions). If you like to "eyeball" positions and dimensions rather than specifying them numerically, the ruler tickmarks are now accurate. You don't have to double check with the Measurements palette or the Item Specifications dialog box.

Comma Tab

A new Comma tab stop has been added to the QuarkXPress environment. The Comma tab stop works identically to the Decimal tab stop except that it uses a comma instead of a period. This is most useful for non-North American users who use a comma to indicate a decimal.

Incremental Layering

You can hold down the Option key while selecting the Item menu. The Send to Back and Send to Front commands become Send Backward and Bring Forward respectively.

Similarly, you can hold the Command-Option-Shift key combination while clicking an object with the Content tool to select the object regardless of how deep within the layer hierarchy it resides. The number of mouse clicks determines the object's level; one click selects a depth of one layer deep, a second click selects an object on the next deeper layer, and so forth.

New Color Models

Two new process color models—Focoltone and Trumatch—have been added to QuarkXPress 3.1. Both of these models are process-color matching systems. The Pantone color model, in comparison, is a spot-color matching system.

The Focoltone matching system is widely used in Western Europe and is comprised of 763 colors. The Focoltone color numbering system is just as indecipherable as the one used by Pantone.

The Trumatch color matching system is comprised of more than 2,000 colors, arranged by gradations and numbered in a manner that is easy to follow. The numbering system follows the color spectrum, so it is quite intuitive to use. The biggest advantage of the Trumatch system is that it allows you to judge the relation of two colors at a glance.

Neither of these color models is of much use, since it is foolhardy to rely on any computer screen for an accurate representation of any printed color. It's simply not accurate enough. This is primarily a result of the differences inherent in the way color is displayed on the computer monitor and the way it is printed on paper. More information is provided in the Working With Color section beginning on page 87.

CHAPTER TWO

Installing QuarkXPress

QuarkXPress v3.1 ships on four 800 KByte floppy disks plus a Registration disk and must be installed using the accompanying installer application. Some of the QuarkXPress program files are compressed on the floppy disks, so you can't simply copy the files to your hard disk drive.

Quark ships two different versions of Quark-XPress: an *updater* version for the installed user base and an *installer* version for new users. Both versions are installed in the same way, although some of the file names may be different.

Resource Requirements

QuarkXPress requires a Macintosh Plus or later with a hard disk drive, an 800 KByte floppy disk drive, and at least 2 MBytes of RAM (4 MBytes of RAM for use with System 7).

A color monitor and at least an 8-bit display card are required if you will be working with color. QuarkXPress does not dither color values to representative tones of gray on a monochrome display. A printer is also required for printed output.

System Software 6.0.5 or later is required and System 7 is fully supported. Some of the more advanced QuarkXPress's features require System 7.

A typical QuarkXPress installation requires a minimum of 4 MBytes of hard disk drive space, not including your document files.

The Installation Process

You can use these steps to install QuarkXPress and its associated files.

1. Insert the QuarkXPress disk labelled "Program Disk 1" in your floppy disk drive.

2. Double-click on the QuarkXPress® Installer icon. The Installer's welcome dialog box will be displayed.

3. Click the **Continue** button. The Product Registration dialog box, shown in Figure 10, will be displayed.

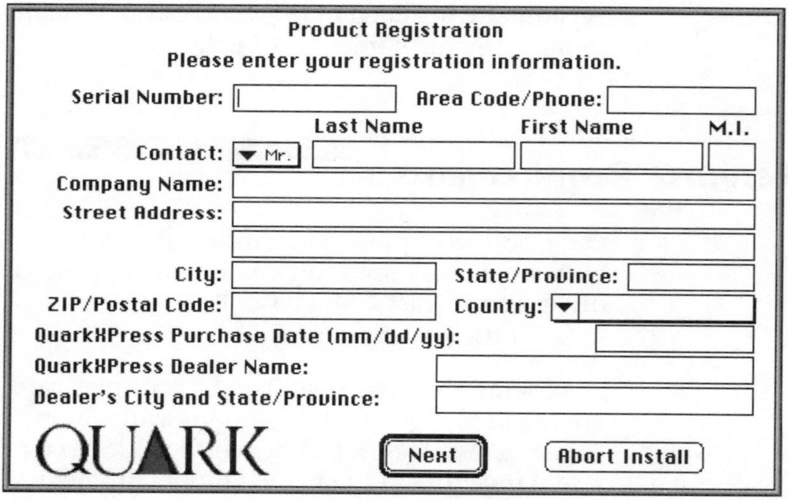

Figure 10   Production Registration dialog box.

4. Enter the appropriate information in the available fields.

5. Click the **Next** button. The System Information dialog box, shown in Figure 11, appears.

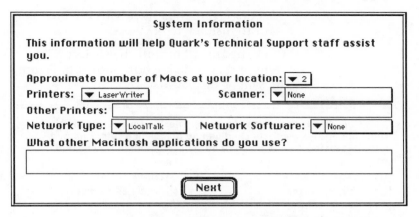

Figure 11   System Information dialog box.

6. Select the appropriate items from the available pop-up menus and enter the appropriate information in the available fields.

7. Click the **Next** button. The User Information Survey dialog box will be displayed.

8. Select the appropriate items from the available pop-up menus and enter the appropriate information in the available fields.

9. Click the **Next** button. The QuarkXPress Installer dialog box will be displayed.

10. Click the **OK** button to begin the installation process. Alternatively, if you need to change any of the information you provided, click the appropriate button to recall its associated information dialog box.

11. Insert the supplied Registration Disk when prompted. Your registration information will be written to the disk and the disk will then

be ejected. The QuarkXPress Installation dialog box will be displayed.

12. Click the **OK** button. The Install as dialog box will be displayed.

13. Select or create the folder within which you want to install QuarkXPress.

14. Click the **Install** button. The Select XTensions and Files dialog box, shown in Figure 12, will be displayed.

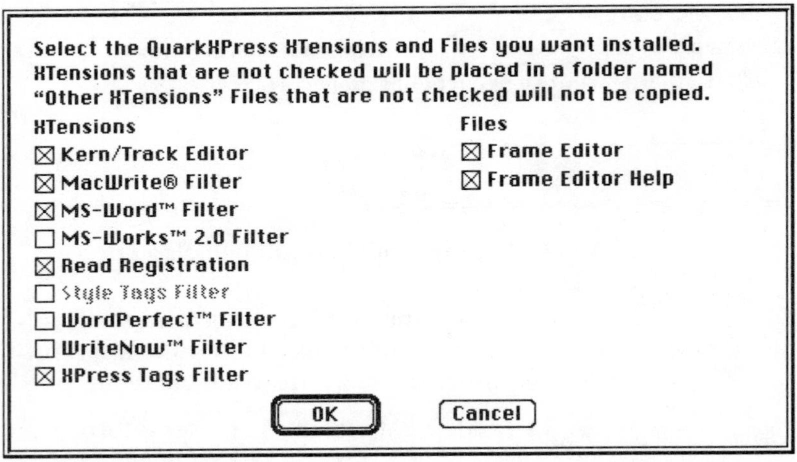

Select the QuarkXPress XTensions and Files you want installed.
XTensions that are not checked will be placed in a folder named
"Other XTensions" Files that are not checked will not be copied.

XTensions

☒ Kern/Track Editor
☒ MacWrite® Filter
☒ MS-Word™ Filter
☐ MS-Works™ 2.0 Filter
☒ Read Registration
☐ Style Tags Filter
☐ WordPerfect™ Filter
☐ WriteNow™ Filter
☒ XPress Tags Filter

Files

☒ Frame Editor
☒ Frame Editor Help

[OK] [Cancel]

Figure 12   Select XTensions and Files dialog box.

15. Check the checkboxes associated with the XTensions and Files you wish to install.

   • These items are the import and export filters, auxiliary files, and the standard set of XTensions.

   • None of these items are required for QuarkXPress to run, but they add functionality to the program.

   • The best approach is usually to add only those filters, files, and XTensions that you will be using on a regular basis.

16. Click the **OK** button. You will be prompted to insert the other disks.

17. Insert the proper disks when prompted.

18. The Select Other XTensions dialog box, shown in Figure 13, will be displayed.

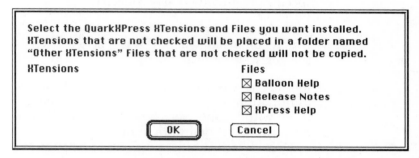

Select the QuarkHPress HTensions and Files you want installed. HTensions that are not checked will be placed in a folder named "Other HTensions" Files that are not checked will not be copied.

HTensions   Files
                                    ☒ Balloon Help
                                    ☒ Release Notes
                                    ☒ HPress Help

            [OK   ]   (Cancel)

Figure 13   Select Other XTensions dialog box.

19. Check the checkboxes associated with the items you wish to install.

    • These items will be placed in a new folder named Other XTensions that will be created within your QuarkXPress installation folder.

    • Only XTensions, Auxiliary Files, and Filters that are placed in the same folder as the QuarkXPress program icon will be available during your work session. Items that are placed within the Other XTensions folder or anywhere else on the hard disk outside of the QuarkXPress folder will not be available.

20. Click the **OK** button. When the process is finished a dialog box notifying you that the installation process was successful appears.

21. Click the **OK** button. The installation process is complete, and QuarkXPress will have been installed with a minimal memory partition.

The Registration Disk

When the QuarkXPress installer program saves your registration information to disk, you should be aware that some information that you did not specifically provide is also collected.

A configuration record of the Macintosh on which you install QuarkXPress is also written to the Registration disk.

Rumors have long circulated about what specific information is collected and why it was being taken without the user's knowledge. The Macintosh configuration information is probably used by Quark's technical support staff to help resolve compatibility problems.

Nevertheless, you may consider this to be discourteous and maybe even invasive. The information probably helps enhance Quark Inc.'s marketing and technical support services, but the information should not be collected without the user's knowledge and express permission.

When you return your Registration disk to Quark, you receive a 90 day limited warranty and you are enrolled in Quark's 90 day service plan.

CHAPTER THREE

QuarkXPress Basics

If you work with multi-page process color documents or if your design-intensive publications require the highest degree of typographic control available, QuarkXPress is arguably the best tool for the job currently available.

This chapter will introduce you to the basic functionality and interface of QuarkXPress.

Preferences

When you first launch QuarkXPress, the Menu bar appears, and you are not prompted to immediately open an existing document or create a new one as you are in some programs.

The first time you launch QuarkXPress is a good time to set the program's defaults, or preferences.

The program's preferences allow you to customize your work environment. QuarkXPress comes with a set of default settings that will be used unless you specifically change them.

You can set all of QuarkXPress's preferences by using the commands available from the Prefer-

ences hierarchical menu on the Edit menu, as
shown in Figure 14.

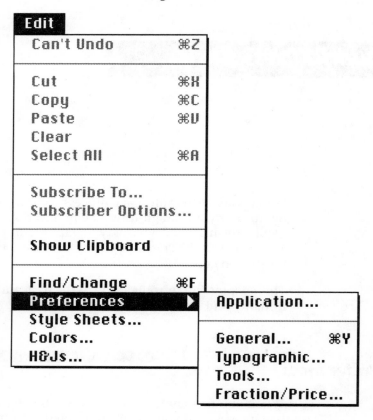

Figure 14   Preferences hierarchical menu.

Application Preferences

You set the QuarkXPress Application preferences
by selecting the Application... command from
the Preferences hierarchical menu on the Edit
menu. The Application preference settings are
discussed in detail in the What's New in Quark-
XPress v3.1? chapter, beginning on page 5.

General Preferences

Selecting the General... command from the Preferences hierarchical menu on the Edit menu causes the General Preferences dialog box, shown in Figure 15, to be displayed.

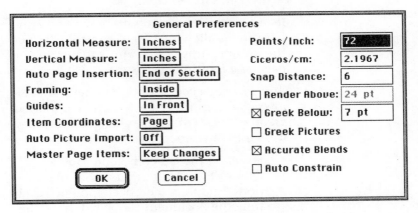

Figure 15   General Preferences dialog box.

Here is a list of the settings available in the General Preferences dialog box.

- *Horizontal Measure* and *Vertical Measure* are pop-up menus to specify the measurement system(s) you want to use. Options are Inches, Inches Decimal, Picas, Points, Millimeters, Centimeters, and Ciceros. You can specify a different measurement system for both the Horizontal and Vertical measures.

- *Auto Page Insertion* is a pop-up menu used to specify where subsequent linked text is placed when the first text box is filled. Options are provided for End of Story, End of Section, End of Document, and Off.

- *Framing* is a pop-up menu containing two items—Inside and Outside—that control whether a frame for a text or picture box falls on the outside or the inside of the box.

- *Guides* is a pop-up menu that contains two items that determine where the non-printing ruler guides appear on the page relative to opaque elements. Options are provided for Behind and In Front.

- *Item Coordinates* is a pop-up menu that contains items allowing you to control whether the non-printing guides apply to a single page or a multiple-page spread.

- *Auto Picture Import* is a pop-up menu that allows you to control how to handle imported graphic images that have changed since they were initially imported.

  - Selecting the On command causes QuarkXPress to check if any of the imported graphics have been modified each time the document is opened. If so, the new version is automatically imported.

  - Selecting the On (verify) command causes QuarkXPress to prompt you for verification before automatically importing a modified graphic image.

  - Selecting the Off command disables the automatic importing of any graphic images that have been modified.

- *Master Page Items* is a pop-up menu that allows you to specify what action QuarkXPress takes if you modify master page elements while in document view.

  - Selecting the Keep Changes option retains any local changes you make to a master page.

  - Selecting the Delete Changes option causes all the master items on an affected page to be deleted and replaced with the original master page items. This allows you to basically reset a document page with the established master page items.

- *Points/Inch* is a field that represents the number of points that comprise an inch. PostScript defines an inch as having 72 points. Traditionally, however, an inch contains 72.27 points. You can use this field to alter the points-per-inch measurement.

- *Ciceros/cm* is a field that allows you to specify the number of ciceros that are contained in a centimeter. A cicero is a unit of measure commonly used in Western Europe; it uses a different size point measurement (a cicero contains 12 points, but the points are a little larger). This field's value is used only if you are using the cicero measurement system.

- *Snap Distance* is a field that allows you to specify the distance (in points) at which the guides begins to exert snap pressure on any object in the document.

- *Render Above* is a checkbox and field that, when checked, allows you to specify a minimum point size for rendering type within the document. This feature works only with Type 3 PostScript fonts.

- *Greek Below* is a checkbox and field that, when checked, allows you to specify a maximum point size for greeking text within the document. Greeked text appears on the screen as a gray bar.

- *Greek Pictures* is a checkbox that, when checked, displays all pictures within the document as gray boxes. This considerably speeds up screen redrawing.

- *Accurate Blends* is a checkbox that, when checked, causes color blends to be displayed accurately, but slowing screen redraw.

- *Auto Constrain* is a checkbox that, when checked, allows you to use the automatic constraint techniques that determined the relationships between parent and child boxes in earlier versions of QuarkXPress. If you are unfamiliar with parent and child box constraints, count your blessings and leave this checkbox unchecked.

Typographic Preferences

under Character

You set the QuarkXPress Typographic preferences by selecting the Typographic... command from the Preferences hierarchical menu on the Edit menu, causing the Typographic Preferences dialog box—shown in Figure 16—to appear.

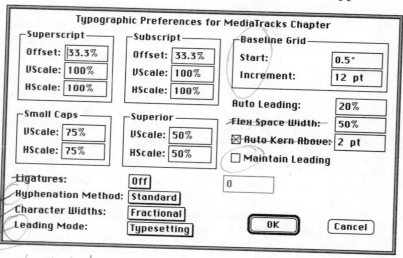

Hyphenation Method
Leading Mode
Baseline Grid
Leading

under Paragraph!

Figure 16   *Typographic Preferences dialog box.*

Controls are provided to customize the typographic characteristics of Superscript, Subscript, Small Caps, and Superior characters. You can specify a vertical scale (VScale) and horizontal

QuarkXPress Rapid Reference

scale (HScale) and an Offset value for Superscript
and Subscript characters.

HScale and *VScale* values determine how tall and
wide the characters are based on a percentage of
the base typeface. A good general value is 75%.

The *Offset* value determines how far away from
the baseline the characters will appear.

The baseline grid is the underlying grid for your
document that ensures that lines of multiple columns will line up with each other horizontally.
You can control whether a text block aligns to
the grid based on its paragraph style, and two
Baseline Grid controls are provided.

- *Start* is a field that contains a value that specifies where the grid begins on the page, measured vertically from the top of the page.

- *Increment* is a field that contains a value that
  specifies the distance between horizontal
  grid lines on the page. In most cases, the value in this field should be set to the leading
  value of your body copy.

The *Auto Leading* value determines the leading in
your document based on a percentage of the
largest typeface on a single line. Be careful ad-
justing this value—any change you make is global to the document; there is no way to change
the auto leading value for a single paragraph.

The *Leading Mode* pop-up menu allows you to
specify a way of measuring leading. Two options
are available: Word Processing and Typesetting.
There is no reason—ever—to use the Word Processing leading mode. The Typesetting option
measures leading from baseline to baseline.

The *Auto Kern Above* checkbox and field allows
you to use the kerning pairs that are built into
the font you are using. The field is provided so

you can limit automatic kerning to specific type sizes. There is really no need to enable automatic kerning below 10 points or so in most fonts.

The *Character Widths* pop-up menu provides two ways to display and print text: Integral and Fractional. The Fractional option employs the true widths of all characters, as defined by the typographer who designed the typeface, and should always be used to maintain the typeface's integrity.

More information on the Typographic preferences is provided in the What's New in QuarkXPress v3.1? chapter, beginning on page 13.

Tools Preferences

You can change the settings for any of the Tool Palette's tools by selecting the Tools... command from the Preferences hierarchical menu on the Edit menu, causing the Tool Preferences dialog box to appear, as shown in Figure 17.

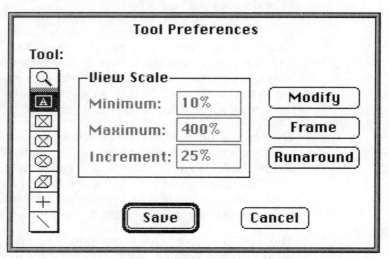

Figure 17   Tool Preferences dialog box.

You can change a tool's default settings by selecting the tool's icon in the left portion of the dialog box and then clicking on one of the three available tool attribute buttons.

Clicking the **Modify** button causes the Item Specifications dialog box for the selected tool to be displayed, as the example for the Text Box tool shown in Figure 18.

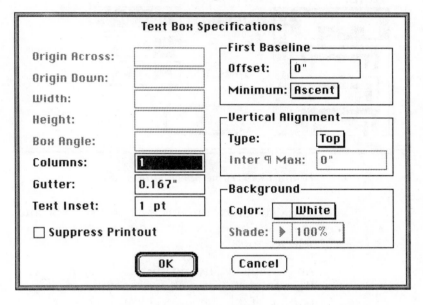

Figure 18   Text Box Specifications dialog box.

The Item Specifications dialog box for the tools will vary from tool to tool. You can alter any value in the dialog box that is not disabled.

You can use this dialog box to change the number of columns, gutter, and text inset of a text box and modify the dimensions and angle of a picture box, for example.

Default alignment, baseline, and background attributes can also be set for each of the tools.

Clicking the **Frame** button causes the Frame
Specifications dialog box to appear, as shown in
Figure 19.

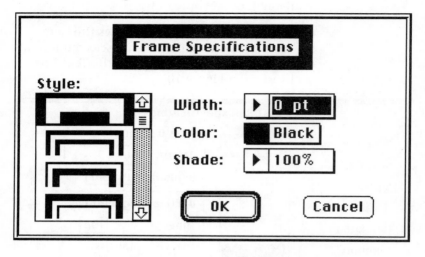

Figure 19   Frame Specifications dialog box.

This dialog box contains style, width, color, and
shade attributes for any frame created with the
selected tool.

An example of any modifications you make to
the frame attribute will appear within the top
portion of the Frame Specifications dialog box,
surrounding the dialog box title.

Clicking the **Runaround** button causes the Runaround Specifications dialog to be displayed.

You can use this dialog box to specify the offset
(measured in points) on all four sides of the text
runaround attribute.

This is a very powerful, yet easy-to-miss feature
of QuarkXPress. It is possible to set a different
offset for each of the different tools. For the various Graphic Box tools, the offset value becomes
a Text Outset specification.

Page Elements

When you first launch QuarkXPress you are not automatically prompted to open an existing document or create a new one, as you are in some layout and design programs.

You create a new document within QuarkXPress by first determining the document's specification, that is, the basic dimensions and orientation of the pages that will comprise it.

Begin the process of creating a new QuarkXPress document by selecting the New command from the File menu. The New dialog box, shown in Figure 20, will be displayed.

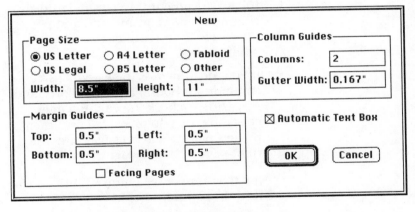

Figure 20   New dialog box.

You determine the document's basic structure with these steps.

1.   Specify a page size by clicking the appropriate **Page Size** radio button.

   •   Alternatively, you can click the **Other** Page Size radio button and enter a width and height dimension for the page size in the provided fields.

- You can use the **Other** Page Size radio button to define a page that is up to 48 inches wide by 48 inches tall. Note that the Page Size dimensions you specify in the New dialog box refers to the size of the finished *pages* of your document, not the size of the *paper* or other media to which you are printing.

2. Specify the margins for your document by entering the appropriate values in the four Margin Guides fields in the lower left portion of the dialog box.

3. Decide whether your document pages will be single- or double-sided and set the **Facing Pages** checkbox appropriately.

   - If your document is to be single-sided—common for letters, memos, and posters—leave the **Facing Pages** checkbox unchecked.

   - If your document is to be double-sided—common for books, annual reports, and magazines—check the **Facing Pages** checkbox. In a double-sided document, the left page (the *verso* page) *faces* the right page (the *recto* page).

4. Specify the number of columns for the document in the Columns field.

5. Specify the width of the gutter—the amount of blank space between column guides—for each page of the document in the Gutter Width field.

   - A gutter setting most often refers to the amount of space added to the inside page margins of a document. This is not true in QuarkXPress. In QuarkXPress, the gutter refers to the amount of space between the non-printing column guides within a multi-column document.

6. Check the **Automatic Text Box** checkbox if you want each page of the document to automatically contain an empty text box.

7. Click the **OK** button. The document window will appear, like the one shown in Figure 21.

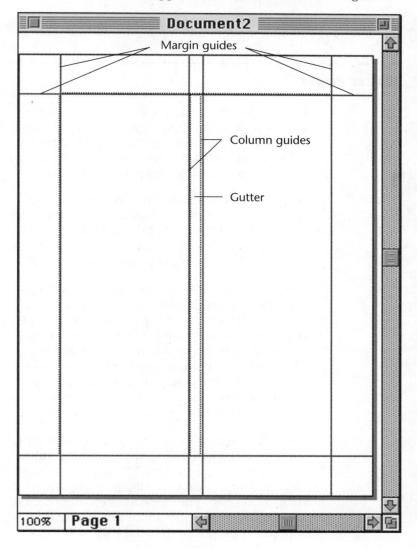

Figure 21   Single-sided document window.

Note that column guides are non-printing and they do not limit in any way what you can do on the pages of your document. Their only functions are to serve as visual guides. When you select the Snap to Guides command from the View menu, rules, text boxes, and graphic boxes all snap to the column guides.

Master Pages

QuarkXPress's master pages contain elements that appear on multiple pages within your document. A rule that you want to appear between two columns on each page of your document, for example, would be a master page element.

Single-sided documents have one master page for the entire document, since there are no left or right pages. Double-sided documents that use facing pages have two master pages: one for the left pages and one for the right pages.

Most other publishing programs such as Page-Maker and FrameMaker use master pages as a sort of transparent overlay on each document page. In these programs, you can turn off the master page information for any specific page. The master page information, however, cannot be altered within these programs and you cannot select the master page elements you want to appear independently of the other elements.

QuarkXPress handles master pages (and their associated elements) differently than most other publishing programs. QuarkXPress master page elements appear on every document page as editable elements—you can edit or change them in any way you see fit. In addition, QuarkXPress supports multiple master pages; up to 127 master pages per document.

Your first master page (or pages in the case of a double-sided document with facing pages) is created for you automatically when you create a new document. This master page is called Master A in single-sided documents and L-Master A (for the left page) and R-Master A (for the right page) in double-sided documents.

You can display the master page(s) of a document in any of three ways.

- Double-click on the Master Page icon in the Document Layout palette.

- Select the Master Page item from the Display hierarchical menu on the Page menu.

- Select the page number in the Page pop-up menu in the lower-left corner of the document window.

Master Guides

Column and margin guides that appear on a master page are called master guides. You can change the margin and column guide settings for your master page(s) at any time with the following set of steps.

1. Select the Master Guides command from the Page menu. The Master Guides dialog box, shown in Figure 22, will be displayed.

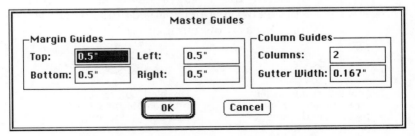

Figure 22   Master Guides dialog box.

2. Specify the new margins for your master page by entering the appropriate values in the four Margin Guides fields.

3. Specify the number of columns for the master page in the Columns field.

4. Specify the width of the gutter—the amount of blank space between column guides—for the master page in the Gutter Width field.

5. Click the **OK** button to apply your changes to the current master page.

Note that any changes you make affect only the current master page. If you use QuarkXPress's multiple master page capability, however, you can have up to 127 different sets of margins and columns—one for each master page—within your document.

Automatic Text Link

When a master page is displayed, the Automatic Text Link icon appears in the upper-left corner of the document window. This is one of the visual feedback devices offered by QuarkXPress to inform you that a master page is displayed.

QuarkXPress's automatic text linking feature allows you to establish a link between text boxes in your document. The state of this function, as indicated by the display of the Automatic Text Link icon, is always either enabled (linked) or disabled (broken) as shown in Figure 23.

Enabled icon represents an automatically linked text box in document

Disabled icon represents a broken automatic link to a text box in document

Figure 23   Automatic Text Link icons.

The Automatic Text Link Box is a text box that is linked through the automatic text link function. Text that overflows an automatic text link in a text box on one page automatically flows into a linked text box on subsequent pages.

You can create an automatic text link manually with these steps.

1. Double-click on the Master Page icon in the Document Layout palette.

2. Select the Linking tool on the Tool palette.

3. Click on the Automatic Text Link icon in the upper-left corner of the document window.

4. Click within the text box you want automatically linked. A Linking Arrow will appear between the Automatic Text Link icon and the linked text box.

Similarly, you can disable an automatic text link manually with these steps.

1. Double-click on the Master Page icon in the Document Layout palette.

2. Select the Unlinking tool on the Tool palette.

3. Click on the Automatic Text Link icon in the upper-left corner of the document window. The Linking Arrow will appear.

4. Click on the end of the Linking Arrow. The automatic text link will be broken and the text box will turn into a standard master page text box.

Note that if you break the automatic text link of a text box on a master page with the above steps, only the specific link selected will be broken. All successive links to other text boxes will be retained. The link will be maintained between the successive text boxes until each link is specifically broken using the steps outlined above.

Automatic Page Numbers

Headers, footers, rules, and graphics that repeat throughout your document are good candidates for master page items. So are automatic page numbers. Here's how to create them.

1. Double-click on the Master Page icon in the Document Layout palette.

2. Select the Text Box tool on the Tool palette.

3. Create a text box on the master page where you want the page numbers to appear on your document pages.

4. Press Command-3 to enter the page number placeholder. The page number placeholder (<#>) will appear.

5. Apply any formatting characteristics or additional text to the text box that contains the page number placeholder.

Ruler Guides

QuarkXPress's ruler guides are the electronic equivalent of the blueline guides found on paste-up boards. Both tools are useful for aligning elements on the page.

You can add vertical or horizontal ruler guides within QuarkXPress by clicking in either of the rulers and dragging the ruler guide out onto the page, placing it wherever you like.

Ruler guides do not ordinarily cross a multiple-page spread. You can work around this limitation with these steps.

1. Clicking on the ruler guide that you want to extend across a multiple-page spread.

2. Drag the ruler guide onto the pasteboard.

3. Deselect the ruler guide by clicking any-where else within the document window.

4. Reselect the ruler guide by clicking on it.

5. Drag the ruler guide back onto the page wherever you like.

You can move any ruler guide by clicking on the guide and dragging it to a new location. When you move a ruler guide, its position is dynamical-ly updated in the Measurements palette.

You can remove any ruler guide by clicking on the guide and dragging it back to the ruler.

Layers

Like most publishing and drawing software pro-grams, QuarkXPress handles multiple page ele-ments by layering them. Every page element—picture boxes, text boxes, rules, and the like—is assigned its own layer based on the order in which it was added to the page.

The first item placed on the page is on the lowest layer; successive items that you add are placed on successively higher layers with the last item placed on the page occupying the highest layer.

Layers within QuarkXPress have little, if any ef-fect, on page elements *unless the elements overlap*.

You can use the Bring to Front and Send to Back commands on the Item menu to control the way objects overlap each other. This is the common convention used within most publishing and drawing software programs.

QuarkXPress offers the additional feature of be-ing able to send page elements through the layering hierarchy one layer at a time by holding down the Option key while selecting the Send Backward and Bring Forward commands from the Item menu.

Navigation

You can navigate throughout your document by using the familiar Macintosh scroll bars, of course, but QuarkXPress offers several more powerful navigation tools.

QuarkXPress's Live Scroll and Page Grabber Hand, described on page 7, can be used to enhance your traditional scrolling-type movements through your document.

QuarkXPress's intelligent screen zoom feature, described on page 19, can be used to display your document at various levels of magnification.

If you have an extended keyboard, you can use Command-Page Down and Command-Page Up to navigate through your document one page at a time. You can use Control-Shift-K and Control-Shift-L on standard keyboards.

You can navigate directly to a specific page of your document in any of three ways.

- Double-click on the Page icon in the Document Layout palette.

- Select the Go to... command from the Page menu and specify the page number in the dialog box that appears. Alternatively, you can issue the Go to... command from the keyboard with Command-J.

- Select the page number in the Page pop-up menu in the lower-left corner of the document window.

Palettes

QuarkXPress's palettes are actually floating windows that always appear on top of any document windows. These palettes can be repositioned anywhere on the screen by dragging them. They can be hidden by clicking their close boxes.

Tool Palette

The Tool palette, shown in Figure 24, contains the basic QuarkXPress tools that you use for creating picture and text boxes and lines. Rotating and linking tools are also provided.

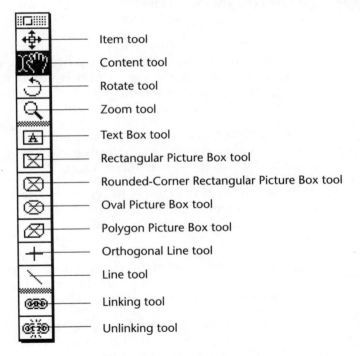

Item tool
Content tool
Rotate tool
Zoom tool
Text Box tool
Rectangular Picture Box tool
Rounded-Corner Rectangular Picture Box tool
Oval Picture Box tool
Polygon Picture Box tool
Orthogonal Line tool
Line tool
Linking tool
Unlinking tool

Figure 24   Tool palette.

Use the Item tool to select and move elements on the page. When this tool is selected, the cursor becomes an Arrow.

The cursor changes to a Four-Headed Arrow when positioned over an element that was created with one of QuarkXPress's Item creation tools.

The cursor turns into a Pointing Hand when it is positioned over a handle of an active element anywhere on the page.

You can move an item without selecting the Item tool by holding down the Command key. This temporarily activates the Item tool until you release the Command key.

Use the Content tool to insert or edit text within a text box. The cursor changes into an I-beam when you place it over a text box.

When you place the cursor over a picture box with the Content tool selected, it changes into the Hand cursor. You can use the Content tool to move graphic items within the picture box when the cursor is in this state.

Use the Rotate tool to rotate any selected element or group of elements on the page. Selecting this tool, turns the cursor into a Target.

When you move the mouse, the cursor changes into an Arrowhead and indicates the direction of the rotation around the target point.

Selecting the Zoom tool enables you to change the magnification scale with which you are viewing the document. When this tool is selected, the cursor changes into the Magnifying Glass.

You can use the Text Box tool to create a box anywhere on the page that will contain text. When you select this tool, the cursor turns into the Crosshair (the Item Creation pointer).

Select any of the four Picture Box tools to create a box on the page that will contain a graphic imported from outside of QuarkXPress.

Each of the tools work similarly, except for the corners of the boxes they create.

When you select any of these tools, the cursor changes into the Crosshair.

Select the Orthogonal Line tool to draw straight lines that are horizontal or vertical.

Select the Line tool to draw straight lines at any angle. The normal constraint controls apply.

Use the Linking and Unlinking tools to control the automatic flow of text between text boxes. Information on using these tools is provided in the Automatic Text Link section, beginning on page 46.

Measurements Palette

The Measurements palette is continuously updated to provide location, dimension, and other information about any selected element within the document.

This offers a significant advantage in high-volume production situations since it saves numerous trips to the comparable menu commands.

In addition to providing feedback information, you can change the measurements and characteristics of the selected element on the page by clicking on an item within the Measurements palette and changing its values.

The Measurements palette itself changes on a dynamic basis, depending on the type of item—

text box, picture box, or rule—selected within the document window.

Figure 25 shows the three different iterations of the Measurements palette.

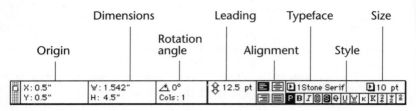

Measurements palette for text boxes.

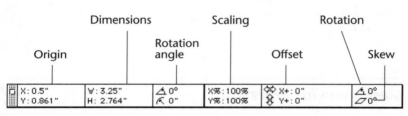

Measurements palette for picture boxes.

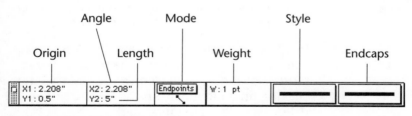

Measurements palette for lines.

Figure 25   Measurements palette.

Document Layout Palette

Unlike the Tool palette and Measurements palette, the Document Layout palette, shown in Figure 26, does not automatically open when you launch QuarkXPress. You can open the Document Layout Palette by selecting the Show Document Layout command from the View menu.

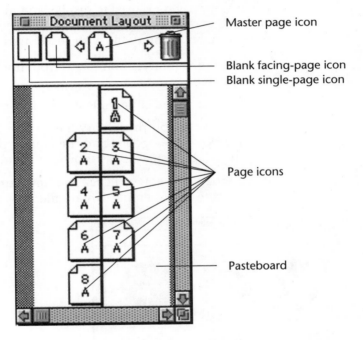

Figure 26   Document Layout palette.

You can use the Document Layout palette to move, delete, and insert pages as well as to create and apply master pages to your document pages.

To move a page, select it and move it where you want it within the palette.

To delete a page, select it and drag it to the trash icon within the palette.

You can create a new master page by dragging the icon representing the kind of master page you want to create—single-page or facing-page—into the master page selection list.

Library Palette

The Library palette is used to display and manipulate the contents of a QuarkXPress Library file. You can open a Library file with these steps.

1. Select the Library... command from the Utilities menu.

2. Navigate to the Library file you wish to open.

3. Double-click on the Library file's name. The Library will be opened and the Library palette will be displayed, as shown in Figure 27.

4. Alternatively, you can click the **New** button to create a new, empty Library file.

Figure 27   Library palette.

You can add up to 2,000 items in each Library file and QuarkXPress allows you to open up to seven Libraries at a time.

Libraries can be used to store any sort of page element—picture boxes, rules, text boxes, and even groups of objects—in a separate file.

TIFF and EPS formatted graphic images are stored a little differently in a QuarkXPress Library file. In the case of these sometimes very complex graphic images, the Library stores only the link to the graphic image file, rather than the image itself. This helps conserve disk space.

You can add an item from your page to an open Library with these steps.

1. Select the element you want to add to the Library with the Item tool.

2. Drag the element into the Library palette. The cursor turns into the Glasses icon when you move the pointer into the Library palette, and two Arrows indicate the current position within the Library.

3. Drag within the Library palette until the two Arrows indicate the position where you want the element to be placed.

4. Release the mouse button. The page element will be placed within the Library at the indicated position.

   • The page element will appear in the Library palette at a substantially reduced size (unless it is stamp-size graphic image). This is called a *thumbnail*, and it contains all of the item's information.

You can also add (or remove) items by using the Paste (or Cut) commands on the Edit menu.

To move an item within the Library, select it and drag it to a new location within the palette.

You can add an item from an open Library to your Document with these steps.

1. Select the Library item you want to add to your document with the Item tool.

2. Drag the item into the document window.

3. Release the mouse button. The Library item will be placed within the document window and can be repositioned as necessary.

You can assign a label to a Library item by double-clicking on the item and entering the label's name in the dialog box that appears.

The labels you assign in this manner appear in the pop-up menu in the upper-left portion of the Library palette.

New Palettes

Palettes that are new to QuarkXPress v3.1—Trap Information Palette, Style Sheets Palette, and Colors Palette—are discussed in the New Palettes section of Chapter 1, beginning on page 15.

XTensions

XTensions are add-on modules that add functionality to QuarkXPress. Some are distributed as freeware and shareware through user groups and online services; others are distributed as commercial products that cost orders of magnitude more than QuarkXPress itself.

It is beyond the scope of this book to provide in-depth information about XTensions. Suffice it to say that all you need to do to use an XTension is to place it in the same folder on your hard disk drive as the QuarkXPress program icon.

CHAPTER FOUR

Working With Text

QuarkXPress has some powerful word processing features, but it is a design tool and usually not the best choice for editing text.

Writing and editing complex passages of text within QuarkXPress can be very slow, even on the fastest Macintosh models. This is mostly a result of the processing power (and time) necessary to support complex hyphenation, justification, and kerning settings.

QuarkXPress works very well with Microsoft Word's style sheets, and that product seems to be the word processor of choice for most Quark-XPress users.

Importing Text

You can import formatted or unformatted text and word processing files into your QuarkXPress documents. It's generally a good idea to use a word processor that is supported by one of QuarkXPress's filters to create, edit, and format your text using the word processor's style sheets. Then *import* the file into QuarkXPress.

Because Microsoft Word's style sheets are directly supported by QuarkXPress, the examples used in this chapter assume the use of formatted Microsoft Word documents. In most cases you are best served by creating, editing, and formatting your text within Microsoft Word and importing the files into your QuarkXPress document.

Use these steps to import a formatted word processing file into your QuarkXPress document.

1. Select the Content tool from the Tool palette.

2. Click in the text box into which you want to import the text. The text box will be selected and handles will appear on its borders.

3. Reposition the cursor within the text box to reflect where you want the text to be imported, if necessary.

4. Select the Get Text... command from the File menu. The Get Text dialog box, shown in Figure 28, will be displayed.

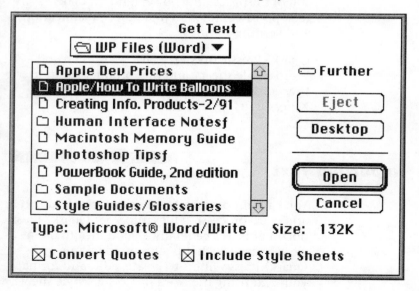

Figure 28   *Get Text dialog box.*

5. Select the file you want to import from the scrolling list.

   - Only files recognized by one of the installed QuarkXPress filters will be displayed in the scrolling list. The type of the selected file and its size will be displayed below the scrolling list.

6. Check the **Convert Quotes** checkbox if you want QuarkXPress to automatically convert typewriter quotes to typographic quotes.

   - Double hyphens will also be converted to a true em dash if you check the **Convert Quotes** checkbox.

7. Check the **Include Style Sheets** checkbox if you want to include the file's style sheet.

   - This option is available only if you select a Microsoft Word file or an ASCII file that uses XPress Tags formatting and style sheet information.

8. Click the **Open** button. The text will be imported using the settings you specified.

Import Filters

A series of special files, called filters, are included in the QuarkXPress distribution package. QuarkXPress uses these filters to import and export text from a variety of popular word processing formats. Supported file formats include MacWrite, Microsoft Word, Word Perfect, and WriteNow.

These filter files must be installed in the same folder as the QuarkXPress program icon in order to be recognized and available for use within QuarkXPress. If you move unneeded filters to another folder, QuarkXPress will launch faster.

Microsoft Word Filter

By far, the Microsoft Word filter is the most powerful filter provided in the standard QuarkXPress distribution package.

When you import a Microsoft Word file into QuarkXPress with the **Include Style Sheets** checkbox checked, each style will be incorporated into the QuarkXPress style sheet.

As much of Word's formatting information will be included as possible.

Here's a list of how QuarkXPress deals with imported Word files.

- Double-underline and dotted-line underline character styles are ignored.

- The Microsoft Word values for superscripts and subscripts are ignored; the QuarkXPress values are applied instead.

- Expanded and condensed character styles are translated to QuarkXPress tracking values.

- Word's Page Break Before paragraph style control is ignored.

- If you import a Word document that contains style names already used within the QuarkXPress document, the Word styles will not be used, and the QuarkXPress paragraph style information will be applied. In other words, the QuarkXPress paragraph styles take precedence when there is any conflict.

  - Any local character formatting that you have applied within Word, however, will be retained when the document is imported within QuarkXPress.

- Graphics are imported into QuarkXPress as inline graphics.

Character Formatting

QuarkXPress does not support character-based style formatting. You can format any selected characters by selecting commands from the Style menu. The only way to make global changes to character formatting is with the Find/Change command described in the Search and Replace section beginning on page 70.

To format characters within your publication, use these steps.

1. Use the Content tool to select the characters for which you want to change the formatting. You can select as many characters as you wish, but they must all be contiguous.

2. Select the appropriate command from the Style menu to format the selected characters. Refer to the table in Figure 29 for specifics.

Command	Action
Font	Select typeface from hierarchical menu.
Size	Specify size of type, in points.
Type Style	Specify typeface style attribute (bold, italic, small caps, etc.).
Color	Specify a color attribute from the available colors.
Shade	Specify a shade attribute, as a percentage of color saturation.
Horizontal Scale	Specify typeface scale based on a percentage of the base typeface.
Track	Specify a tracking value as a number of units. Each unit is 1/200th of an em.
Baseline Shift	Specify the baseline shift, in points.

Figure 29   Type menu character formatting.

You can also apply character formatting to a selected range of characters by selecting the Character... command from the Style menu and altering the settings within the Character Attributes dialog box, shown in Figure 30.

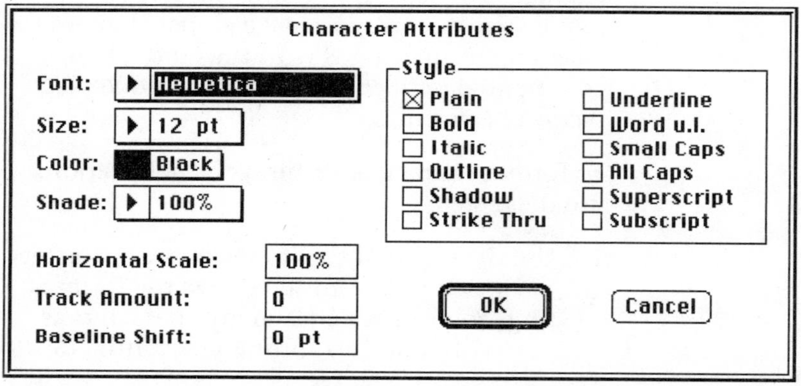

Figure 30   Character Attributes dialog box.

Paragraph Formatting

All of the paragraph formatting information is contained within the document's *style sheet*. The style sheet is a collection of the document's paragraph formatting *styles*. A paragraph's style determines the "look" of the paragraph without affecting its content. Style sheets help assure a high degree of consistency throughout the pages of your document.

Style sheets are very useful because a single style can control all of a paragraph's formatting information—typeface, size, style, alignment, leading, spacing, etc.—and can be applied with a single mouse click. Styles allow you to make global changes in your document by applying or editing the formatting information contained within a style.

The best way to maintain consistency in your document is to remember to *apply a style to every paragraph* in your publication. You can do this in a variety of ways—including importing them from your word processor. Styles allow you to change *every occurrence* of styled paragraphs simply by editing the style definition.

You apply styles to paragraphs within your publication by clicking the Content tool within a paragraph that you want to format and selecting a style from the Style Sheets palette, like the one shown in Figure 31. You can display the Style Sheets palette by selecting the Show Style Sheets command from the View menu.

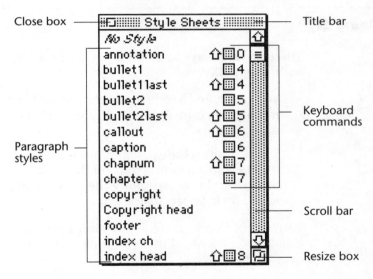

Figure 31   Style Sheets palette.

QuarkXPress is capable of importing styles or formatting tags from word processing documents as you import them within the QuarkXPress document. It is important to remember, however, that QuarkXPress's native style definitions take precedence over any style sheet that is imported from a word processing file.

Sometimes importing styles is very useful, but it is generally easier to define and edit all paragraph styles within QuarkXPress. QuarkXPress offers you significantly greater control over formatting than most word processors.

There is nothing you can do with QuarkXPress's paragraph styles that you cannot do with the various menu commands and their associated dialog boxes. The advantage that using styles offers is that you can change *every occurrence* of styled paragraphs simply by editing the style. *The enormity of that advantage cannot be overstated.*

Defining Styles

There are two ways to define a paragraph style within QuarkXPress.

- You can define a style by entering values and modifying controls within the Style Sheets dialog box; or

- You can format the paragraph visually—using the various commands on the Style menu—and then assigning the style a name in the Style Sheets dialog box.

Both methods offer roughly the same options, although you may find that you prefer one way over the other.

Any styles you define, delete, or edit pertain only to the active document. You can create a default style sheet for QuarkXPress by defining a series of paragraph styles without an open document. The default style sheet is then available in every new document you create within QuarkXPress.

You can create a new paragraph style, using the Style Sheets dialog box method, with these steps.

1. Select the Style Sheets… command on the Edit menu. The Style Sheets dialog box will appear, as shown in Figure 32.

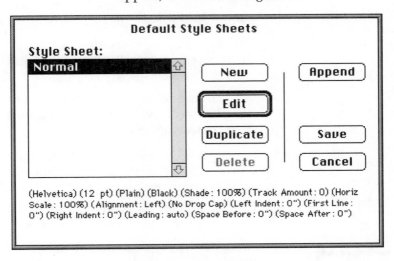

Figure 32   Style Sheets dialog box.

2. Click the **New** button. The Edit Style Sheet dialog box, shown in Figure 33, will appear.

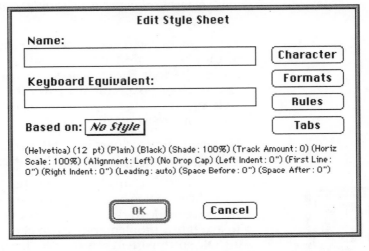

Figure 33   Edit Style Sheet dialog box.

3. Enter the name for the new style in the Name field.

- The style must be named or it will not appear in the Style Sheets palette.

4. Optionally, enter the keyboard equivalent for invoking the style in the Keyboard Equivalent field.

- You can use any of the function keys on the extended keyboard and the number keys on the numeric keypad.

5. Optionally, select an existing style, if available, on which to base the new style from the Based On pop-up menu.

6. Use the table in Figure 34 on page 69 to define the style's formatting characteristics.

- Note that the **Character, Formats, Rules**, and **Tabs** buttons in the Edit Style Sheet dialog box correspond with the Character..., Formats..., Rules..., and Tabs... commands on the Style menu. *The actions initiated by clicking these buttons are identical to the actions initiated by selecting the menu commands.*

- Any changes you make to the style sheet definition are reflected in the lower portion of the Style Sheets dialog box. The nested dialog boxes initially cover the Style Sheets dialog box; you can reposition them anywhere on your screen.

- There is no way to "preview" the effect of a change you make to a style's definition.

- If you click the **Cancel** button in the Style Sheets dialog box, all of the changes you have made to the style will be lost. To avoid this problem, be sure to click the **OK** button after each change that you wish to make permanent.

The table in Figure 34 provides an overview of the controls available directly from within the Edit Style Sheet dialog box.

Button	Control
Character	Displays Character Attributes dialog box; set Font, Size, Color, and Shade via pop-up menus. Specify font styling attributes via standard Style checkboxes. Set Horizontal Scale, Track Amount, and Baseline Shift by entering appropriate values in the fields.
Formats	Displays Paragraph Formats dialog box; set Indents for Left Indent, First Line, and Right Indent by entering values in the fields. Specify Leading by accepting the "auto" default or by entering a value in the field. Specify values for the Space Before and Space After paragraph attributes by entering values in the fields. Check the **Lock to Baseline Grid** checkbox to override paragraph leading and lock the paragraph to the Baseline Grid. Check the **Drop Caps** checkbox and specify values in the Character Count and Line Count fields to add a Drop Cap. Check the **Keep with Next ¶** checkbox to prevent a page or column break between paragraphs. Check the **Keep Lines Together** checkbox and specify values in the Start and End fields to control widows and orphans. Select an Alignment characteristic and Hyphenation and Justification sensitivity from the pop-up menus.
Rules	Displays Paragraph Rules dialog box; check the **Rule Above** or **Rule Below** checkbox to attach a rule to the paragraph style. Checking either checkbox displays a set of controls for Length, Width, Dimensions, Color, and Shade.
Tabs	Displays Paragraph Tabs dialog box; set tabs by clicking in the ruler. Specify a Fill Character by entering a character in the field.

Figure 34   Edit style dialog box button controls.

7. Click the **OK** button in the Edit Style Sheet dialog box. The Style Sheets dialog box remains on the screen.

- At this point you can select any available style to edit (select the name and click the **Edit** button) or you can click the **New** button to create a new paragraph style, again referring to the table in Figure 34 for the button names and the style attribute control parameters.

- You can remove any existing style by selecting the style you want to delete in the Style Sheets dialog box and clicking the **Delete** button.

- You can copy the paragraph styles from any available QuarkXPress document by clicking the **Append** button and selecting the document from which you wish to copy the styles.

8. Click the **Save** button in the Style Sheets dialog box to accept your changes.

Search and Replace

The Find/Change command offered in Quark-XPress is significantly more powerful than that offered by many word processing programs.

Because QuarkXPress's Find/Change command is capable of searching (and replacing) typographic attributes as well as text content, you may find it more productive to do most of your searching and replacing within QuarkXPress.

You can change the default settings for the Find/Change command by modifying any of the controls with no document open within the QuarkXPress environment.

You can use these steps to search and replace text or typographic elements.

1. To search the entire document, make sure that *no* text box is selected.

    - Alternatively, to search a single text box, and all linked text boxes, click in the text box with the Content tool.

2. Select the Find/Change command from the Edit menu. The Find/Change dialog box, shown in Figure 35 will be displayed.

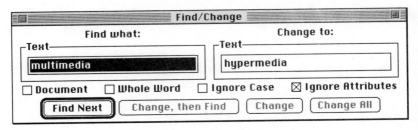

Figure 35   Find/Change dialog box.

3. Enter the text for which you want to search in the Find what field.

4. Enter the complete replacement text in the Change to field.

5. Refer to the table in Figure 36 to set the various checkboxes.

Checkbox	Control
Document	Check to search entire document.
Whole Word	Check to find whole words only.
Ignore Case	Check to find without regard to case.
Ignore Attributes	Check to search without regard to typographic attributes.

Figure 36   Find/Change dialog box checkbox controls.

6. Refer to the table in Figure 37 for an explanation of the available **Find** buttons.

Button	Control
Find Next	Find next occurrence of target.
Change, then Find	Change found occurrence of target and find next occurrence of target.
Change	Change found occurrence of target.
Change All	Change every occurrence of target in specified range.

Figure 37   Find/Change dialog box button controls.

7. Uncheck the **Ignore Attributes** checkbox to search on typographic attributes. The Find/Change dialog box will be extended, as shown in Figure 38.

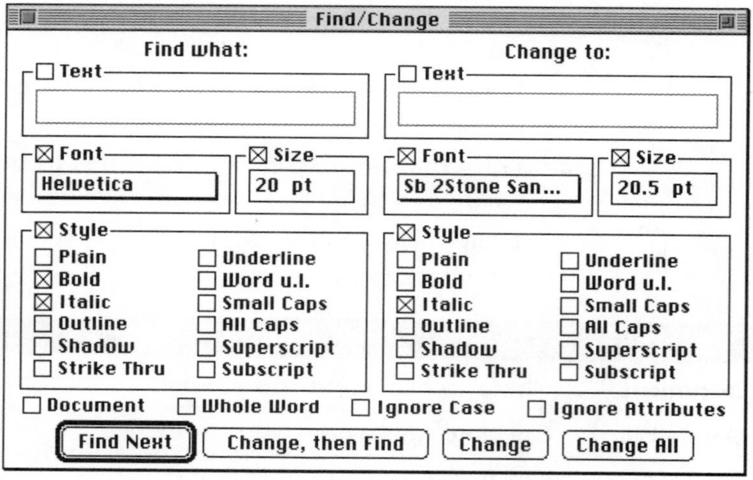

Figure 38   Extended Find/Change dialog box.

8. Specify the Font for which to search.

9. Specify the Size for which to search.

10. Specify the replacement Font by selecting an item from the pop-up menu in the Change to portion of the dialog box.

11. Specify the replacement Size by entering a value in the field.

12. Refer to the table in Figure 36 on page 71 to set the various checkboxes.

13. Refer to the table in Figure 37 on page 72 for an explanation of the available **Find** buttons.

Exporting Text

QuarkXPress is a page layout program, it's not a word processor. It's fine for editing small passages of text, but it's not a writing tool.

If you find that you have to edit a lot of your text, you may find that you have to export it out of QuarkXPress in a format that can be read by your word processor.

Being able to export text is also important in a workgroup environment where writers have to be rewriting existing text while the designer is working on the document's layout.

To export text from QuarkXPress, use these steps.

1. Select the Content tool from the Tool palette.

2. Click within a text box containing the text you want to export.

3. Select the Save Text... command from the File menu. The Save Text dialog box appears.

4. Enter the name under which you want to save the exported text.

5. Click either the **Entire Story** or **Selected Text** radio button.

6. Select the file format under which to save the exported text from the pop-up menu, as shown in Figure 38.

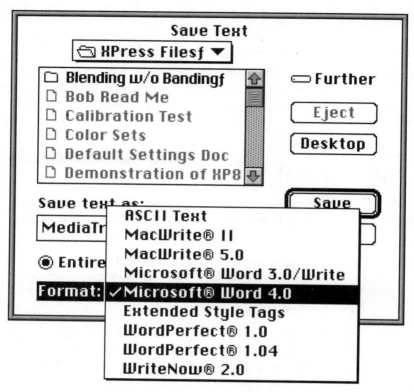

Figure 39   Save Text dialog box.

7. Click the **Save** button.

Be careful about which file format you choose to export text if you will be re-importing the text into QuarkXPress. The Microsoft Word file format supports paragraph format (style sheet) information, but cannot export (or re-import) any local formatting you may have applied.

In certain cases, using XPress Tags may offer a better solution; all formatting will be retained, but the text will be nearly impossible to edit.

CHAPTER FIVE

Working With Graphics

Just as QuarkXPress is not a word processor, neither is it an illustration or drawing program—even though it does offer a frame creation tool and two basic line tools. Most of the graphic elements that you include in your documents will be created in another software program and imported to the QuarkXPress environment.

This chapter provides information about working with graphics—both graphics that you place within your document and graphic elements that you create with QuarkXPress's Line tools.

Importing Graphics

QuarkXPress supports the four major Macintosh graphics file formats.

- *Paint-type* graphics are bitmapped images created by MacPaint-type programs. These images are usually of very low resolution and generally don't print well.

- *Draw-type* graphics are object-oriented images created by MacDraw type-programs. These are also known as PICT-format graphics.

- *TIFF* graphics are images usually created with a scanner. TIFF is an acronym for the Tag Image File Format.

- *EPS* graphics are PostScript images created with PostScript drawing programs like Free-Hand and Illustrator. EPS is an acronym for the Encapsulated PostScript file format.

You can import graphic elements to your document with these steps.

1. Use your graphics program to create the image to be used within your document.

   - It is best to create separate disk files for each graphic in the publication.

2. Create a picture box in your QuarkXPress document to contain the imported graphic.

   - Select one of the Picture Box tools from the Tool palette, described in the Tool Palette section beginning on page 51.

   - Draw a box, beginning in the upper-left corner, to contain the imported graphic.

3. Select the Get Picture ... command from the File menu. The Get Picture dialog box will be displayed, as shown in Figure 40.

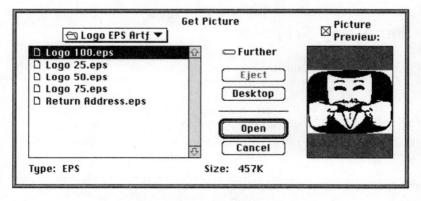

Figure 40   Get Picture dialog box.

4. Navigate to the file containing the graphic you want to import.

5. Select the graphic file you want to import.

   • The file type and its size will be displayed in the lower portion of the dialog box.

6. Click the **Open** button. The graphic will be imported into the picture box.

Manipulating Graphics

You can move an imported graphic image *within its picture box* by selecting the Content tool from the Tool palette, clicking on the graphic image, and dragging it to the desired position.

Move the *picture box and the graphic image it contains* by selecting the Item tool from the Tool palette, clicking on the picture box, and dragging it to the desired position.

Center an imported graphic image *within its picture box* by typing Command-Shift-M.

QuarkXPress allows you to rotate a graphic in fine increments (one one-thousandth of a degree). You can rotate the picture box's frame separately from the graphic image it contains, or you can rotate both elements together.

There are two methods of rotating page elements within QuarkXPress.

• You can enter new Box Angle and Corner Radius values in the Measurements palette (shown in Figure 25 on page 54).

• Alternatively, you can alter the values in the Picture Box Specifications dialog box with the following steps.

1. Select the Item tool from the Tool palette.

2. Double-click on the graphic image you want to rotate. The Picture Box Specifications dialog box, shown in Figure 41, will appear.

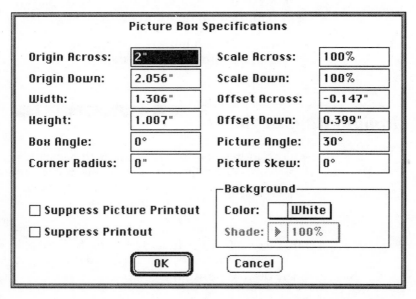

Picture Box Specifications

Origin Across:	2"	Scale Across:	100%
Origin Down:	2.056"	Scale Down:	100%
Width:	1.306"	Offset Across:	-0.147"
Height:	1.007"	Offset Down:	0.399"
Box Angle:	0°	Picture Angle:	30°
Corner Radius:	0"	Picture Skew:	0°

☐ Suppress Picture Printout

☐ Suppress Printout

Background

Color: White

Shade: ▷ 100%

OK   Cancel

Figure 41   Picture Box Specifications dialog box.

3. Enter the value for the graphic's degree of rotation in the Picture Angle field.

   • This is the degree of rotation for the *graphic* within the picture box.

4. Enter the value for the picture box's degree of rotation in the Box Angle field.

   • This is the degree of rotation for the *picture box and the graphic element* it contains, rotated as a single unit.

5. Click the **OK** button. The graphic and/or picture box will be rotated within the document window using the settings you specified in steps 3 and 4.

Rotating the picture box also rotates the graphic image it contains. If you want the picture box (and its frame) rotated, but the graphic they contain straight, use the following set of steps.

1. Follow steps 1–2 in the previous sequence to display the Picture Box Specifications dialog box shown in Figure 41.

2. Enter the value for the picture box's degree of rotation in the Box Angle field.

   • This is the degree of rotation for the *picture box and the graphic element* it contains, rotated as a single unit.

3. Enter the negative value for the value you entered in step 2 for the graphic's degree of rotation in the Picture Angle field.

   • This is the degree of rotation for the *graphic* within the picture box.

   • If you entered 30° in the Box Angle field, enter -30° in the Picture Angle field.

4. Click the **OK** button. The graphic and the picture box will be rotated independently within the document window, resulting in the image shown in Figure 42.

30° Box Angle
0° Picture Angle

30° Box Angle
-30° Picture Angle

Figure 42   *Rotated picture box and graphic.*

Text Runaround

QuarkXPress provides you with a method of controlling the way flowed text wraps around graphics within a document. This is referred to as text runaround and is one of QuarkXPress's most powerful and efficient features.

You can use these steps to specify the text runaround parameters for a text box or picture box within QuarkXPress.

1. Select the Item tool from the Tool palette.

2. Click on the text box or picture box around which you want the text to flow. Handles will appear around the text box or picture box, indicating that it has been selected.

3. Select the Runaround... command from the Item menu.

    • The Runaround Specifications dialog box for the selected element will be displayed, similar to the example shown in Figure 43.

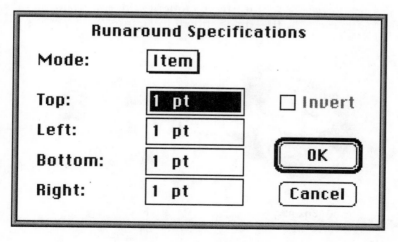

Figure 43   Runaround Specifications dialog box.

4. Refer to the table in Figure 44 to determine the appropriate Runaround Mode to select from the Mode pop-up menu.

Command	Control
None	Available for text boxes and picture boxes. No text is offset, and text flows normally *behind* the selected element. The text offset fields are disabled.
Item	Available for text boxes and picture boxes. Text flows around the *edges of the box* itself, as opposed to what the box contains. Specify a text offset in the four available fields.
Auto Image	Available for picture boxes only. Text flows around the *edges of the image* contained in the picture box, as opposed to the edges of the box itself. Specify a text offset in the four available fields.
Manual Image	Available for picture boxes only. Text flows around the edges of the image contained in the picture box, based on the dimensions of the corners and line segments you modify within the *text runaround polygon*. Specify a text offset in the four available fields.

Figure 44   Runaround Mode pop-up menu commands and controls.

5. Enter values for the *text offset* in the Top, Left Bottom, and Right fields. This is the amount of space to leave between the runaround text and the page element.

6. Optionally, check the **Invert** checkbox to flow text around the inside of a text runaround polygon.

7. Click the **OK** button. The runaround specifications will be applied to the selected text box or picture box.

Examples of various text runarounds are provided in Figure 45.

Runaround mode: None.

Runaround mode: Item.

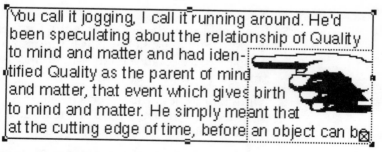

Runaround mode: Auto Image.

Figure 45   Text runarounds.

Anchored Picture Boxes

One of QuarkXPress's most advanced features is its ability to place *anchored picture boxes* within a document. Anchored picture boxes in Quark-XPress are similar in nature to *inline graphics* in other publishing programs.

Anchored picture boxes are embedded within a text block and float as you edit the surrounding text. QuarkXPress adds additional functionality to the concept of inline graphics by supporting *anchored text boxes* as well. They work the same as anchored picture boxes.

Use these steps to convert a picture box into an anchored picture box.

1. Select the Item tool from the Tool palette.

2. Select the picture box containing the graphic image that you want to convert to an anchored picture box.

3. Select the Cut or Copy command from the Edit menu. The picture box and its contents will be placed on the Clipboard.

4. Select the Content tool from the Tool palette.

5. Position the cursor within the text box at the point where you want the anchored picture box to appear.

6. Select the Paste command from the Edit menu. The picture box will be pasted into the document at the cursor position as a *character*, rather than a picture box.

Anchored picture boxes have some limitations.

*   You can anchor boxes only. You cannot anchor other page elements such as rules.

*   You cannot anchor a group of objects.

- You cannot rotate anchored boxes.

- You cannot drag an anchored box to another location within the document.

- You cannot nest anchored boxes, i.e., you cannot place an anchored box inside of another anchored box.

You can modify many of the characteristics of an anchored picture or text box by changing the values and controls in the Anchored Box Specifications dialog box. You display the dialog box by selecting the Item tool from the Tool palette and double-clicking on the anchored box. The Anchored Picture Box Specifications dialog box is shown in Figure 46.

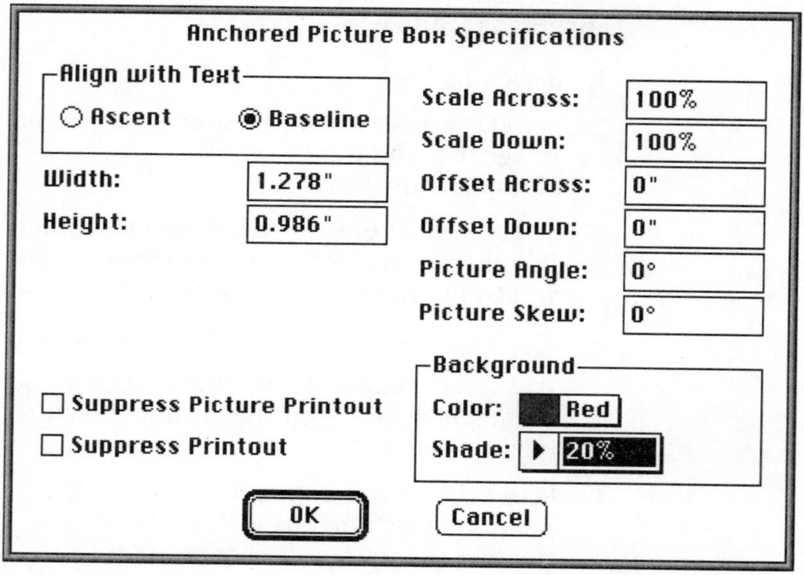

Figure 46   Anchored Picture Box Specifications dialog box.

The controls available for an anchored text box are roughly the same, with the addition of values for number of columns, inset, and gutter.

Using the Line Tools

The QuarkXPress Tool palette provides two Line tools that you can use to draw lines with a variety of weight, style, endcap, and color attributes. The Tool palette and the Line tool and the Orthogonal Line tool are discussed in the Tool Palette section, beginning on page 51.

Use the Orthogonal Line tool to draw straight lines that are perfectly horizontal or vertical. These lines can be of any thickness between 0.001 and 504 points.

You use the Line tool to draw straight lines at any angle. You can create a perfectly horizontal or vertical line with the Line tool by holding down the Shift key as you create the line. Holding down the Shift key while drawing at an angle constrains the angle to 45 or 90 degrees.

You can alter the line's color, shade, weight, and endcap from the controls provided in the Measurements palette as illustrated in Figure 25 on page 54.

You can also alter the line's attributes by changing the values and controls in the Line Specifications dialog box as explained in the following sequence. Either method offers the same results; which one you choose to use depends on your personal preference.

1. Create a line using either of the Line tools on the Tool palette.

   • Select one of the two Line tools from the Tool palette.

   • Click where you want one of the line's endpoints to appear.

   • Keep the mouse button depressed.

- Drag to where you want the other endpoint to appear.

- Release the mouse button.

2. Select the Item tool from the Tool palette.

3. Double-click on the line you want to change. The Line Specifications dialog box, shown in Figure 47, will be displayed.

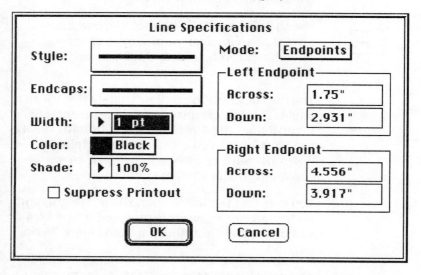

Line Specifications

Style:

Mode: [Endpoints]

Endcaps:

┌─Left Endpoint────
Across: 1.75"
Down: 2.931"

Width: ▶ 1 pt

Color: ■ Black

Shade: ▶ 100%

┌─Right Endpoint────
Across: 4.556"
Down: 3.917"

☐ Suppress Printout

[OK]   [Cancel]

Figure 47   Line Specifications dialog box.

4. Set the attributes for the line with the controls available in the dialog box.

5. Click the **OK** button. The attributes will be applied to the selected line.

QuarkXPress measures line width or line weight as the thickness of the line. The weight of the line is centered on the line itself. In other words, if you specify a 3-point rule, 1.5 points fall on one side of the line and 1.5 points fall on the other side of the line. You can also increase and decrease line weight in one point increments with Command-Shift-> and Command-Shift-<.

Working With Color

QuarkXPress supports both spot color and full, four-color process color. Working with process color can be very complicated, however, and you should always plan color projects with both your service bureau and commercial printer before undertaking a major project.

Spot Color

Adding spot color to your document is a relatively simple process because it requires only one additional printing plate (one plate for each color; most spot color uses call for one color plus black). The color is defined by assigning a pre-mixed ink value to the appropriate objects.

QuarkXPress supports the PANTONE, Trumatch, and Focoltone color models for spot color. The PANTONE color matching system is the oldest and one of the most widely used in the printing industry. Trumatch and Focoltone are explained on page 24.

These color models serve to standardize the way designers, illustrators, ink vendors and manufacturers, and commercial printers specify colors. PANTONE Red 032, for instance, is always exactly the same color red.

Process Color

Process color allows the creation of virtually any color by blending percentages of four separate colors (cyan, magenta, yellow, and black). Using process color in your document requires that you create at least four separate printing plates, one for each color.

QuarkXPress supports the CMYK, RGB, and HSB color models for process color. Unless you have a compelling reason to use one of the other color models, use the CMYK model for your process color work. The CMYK model is the one most commonly used by commercial printers.

Adding Colors

An introduction to QuarkXPress's Colors palette and instructions for adding color to page elements is provided beginning on page 17.

Before you can use a color, you have to add it to the Colors palette with these steps.

1. Close all open documents if you want to create a default Colors palette that will be available to all documents.

2. Select the Colors... command from the Edit menu. The Colors dialog box, shown in Figure 48, will be displayed.

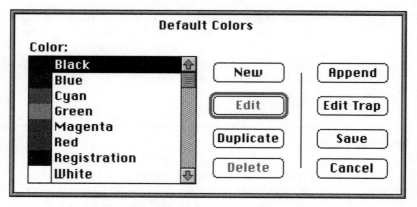

Figure 48   Colors dialog box.

3. Click the **New** button. The Edit Color dialog box, shown in Figure 49, will be displayed.

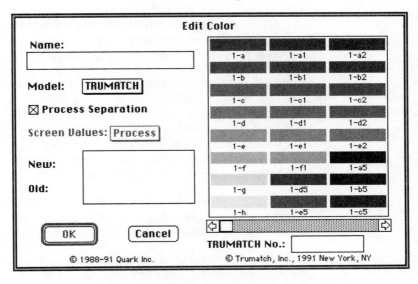

Figure 49   Edit Color dialog box.

4. Select the color model from which you want to add a color from the Model pop-up menu. The Trumatch model is selected in Figure 49.

5. Select the color you want to add from the scrolling panel of color swatches in the right portion of the dialog box.

   • The color's name will be added to the Name field.

   • The color's identification number will appear in the Identification field.

   • A larger swatch of the color will be displayed in the swatch panel in the left portion of the dialog box.

6. Click the **OK** button. The color will be added to both the Colors palette and the Colors dialog box, which remains on the screen.

Trap

An entire book could be written on the process of trapping color on the desktop. This one-page overview is overly simplified and incomplete.

When a color document is printed on a printing press, each color is added one step at a time. With each pass on the press, the paper is likely to shift, and if two colors adjoin each other they may be separated slightly on the paper, resulting in an unwanted, unprinted space. This problem is remedied by overprinting and trapping.

Overprinting is one color printing on top of another color, accomplishing basically the same result as creating a knock out on the bottom color.

Trapping is the process of overprinting two adjoining colors along their borders, allowing the unprinted space to be filled with the additional trap color if the paper shifts on the press. A trap can be accomplished by *choking* the background object (making it smaller) or by *spreading* the foreground object (making it larger).

You can specify how QuarkXPress traps and overprints colors with these steps.

1. Select the Colors... command from the Edit menu. The Colors dialog box, shown in Figure 48 on page 88, will appear.

2. Select a color in the scrolling list.

3. Click the Edit Trap button. The Trap Specifications dialog box for that color will appear.

4. Set the value for the appropriate foreground/background colors using the Automatic, Overprint, and Trap buttons.

5. Click the **OK** button. The trap specifications for the color will be added.

Index

Numerics

adding 88–89
trapping 90
Colors palette 17–19, 88
column guides 44
columns 42
Comma tab stop 23
Content tool 52
Convert Quotes 61
crop marks 10

D

Document Layout palette 55–56
document window 43

E

exporting text 73–74

F

facing pages 42, 44
filters 61–62
Microsoft Word 62
find and change 70–73
flex space 14
Focoltone 24, 87
font selection 20–21
Framing 33

G

Get Edition Now button 4
graphics
importing 75–77
inline 83–84
manipulating 77–79
rotating 77–79
Greek Below 35
Greek Pictures 35
Grid guides 6
Guide Colors buttons 6
Guides 34
gutter 42

H

I

K

L

M

N

navigation 50

O

Off-screen Draw 7
Offset 37
Open Publisher button 5
Orthogonal Line tool 53
overprinting 90

P

Page Grabber Hand 7
page number placeholder 48
page size 41
palettes 15–19, 51–58
Pantone 9, 24, 87
paragraph formatting 64–70
Pasteboard 10
Pasteboard Width field 10
Picture Box tool 53
Picture Preview 20
Points/Inch 35
preferences 31–40
    Application preferences 5–13, 32
    General preferences 33–36
    Tools preferences 38–40
    Typographic preferences 13–14, 36–38
process color 87–88
Professional Color Toolkit 9
Publish and Subscribe 2–5

R

Reg. Marks Offset field 10
registration marks 10
Render Above 35
resource requirements 25–26
RGB 88
Rotate tool 52
Ruler guides 6, 22–23, 48–49

S

Scroll Speed 9
search and replace 70–73
Single Word Justify 21
Snap Distance 35
Snap to Guides 44
spot color 87
spreading 90
style sheets 64–70
    applying 65
    defining 66–70
    importing 65–66
Style Sheets palette 16–17, 65
Subscribe button 3
Subscribe to... command 3
Subscriber options 4–5
System 7 support 1–2

T

Text Box tool 52
text offset 81
text runaround 80–82
thumbnail 57
Tint Percentage 18
Tool palette 51–53
trap 11–13, 15–16, 90
    Auto Amount 11
    Auto Method 11
    Ignore White 12
    Indeterminate 11–12
    Overprint Limit 12
    Process Trap 13
Trap Information palette 15–16
TrueType 2
Trumatch 24, 87, 89
Type 1 PostScript fonts 2

U

Unlinking tool 53

V

X

Z

OTHER BOOKS AVAILABLE IN THE
BUSINESS ONE IRWIN RAPID REFERENCE SERIES:

GUIDE TO ADOBE® ILLUSTRATOR®
Michael Fraase

Upgrade your software or easily use the new revision with this
valuable quick reference! You'll find frustration-saving solutions to
common problems, step-by-step instructions for using each tool,
feature, and ability of the program, and shortcuts and keyboard
equivalents to minimize wasted time.
ISBN: 1-55623-742-1 (paper)

GUIDE TO THE LASERWRITER® FAMILY
Michael Fraase

While many guides are filled with technical jargon, this Rapid
Reference guide clearly describes how to take advantage of the
numerous features of the LaserWriter family. You'll find out how to
get the best output from each printer, avoid paper jams—and easily
clear them when they do occur, select the best paper for use with
the printers, and much more!
ISBN: 1-55623-747-2 (paper)

GUIDE TO MICROSOFT® WORD 5.0
Michael Fraase

Whether you are new to computing or just new to Word, this book's
step-by-step format will guide you in getting the most productivity
from the software. You'll find specific instructions on how to create
memos easily and clearly, compile complex reports quickly, and
much more! You can take advantage of all of Word's capabilities,
including menus, macros, and linking documents, with this
outstanding reference.
ISBN: 1-55623-746-4 (paper)

GUIDE TO SYSTEM 7
Michael Fraase

Optimize the productivity of your System 7 operating system! This
guide lays out all the basics for taking advantage of System 7's
virtual memory, 32-bit addressing, file sharing, and much more.
You'll find all the information you need to get your system up and
running quickly and easily. Instead of wasting time with theoretical
information, you'll locate practical, hands-on solutions to your
computing challenges so you can minimize wasted time.
ISBN: 1-55623-745-6 (paper)

Available at fine bookstores and libraries everywhere.

DUE DATE

JUN 0 8 2000		
JUN 0 8 2000		